Commentary on the Books of Joshua and Ruth

Bible Study Notes and Comments

by David E. Pratte

Available in print at
www.gospelway.com/sales

Commentary on the Books of Joshua and Ruth:
Bible Study Notes and Comments

Revised Edition

© Copyright David E. Pratte, 2010, 2013
Minor revisions 2016
All rights reserved

ISBN-13: 978-1502710178
ISBN-10: 150271017X

Note carefully: No teaching in any of our materials is intended or should ever be construed to justify or to in any way incite or encourage personal vengeance or physical violence against any person.

Front Page Photo
The ruins of ancient Jericho (public domain)

"And the Lord said to Joshua, 'See! I have given Jericho into your hand...'" – Joshua 6:2
"By faith the walls of Jericho fell down after they were encircled for seven days." – Hebrews 11:30

Other Acknowledgements
Unless otherwise indicated, Scripture quotations are generally from the New King James Version (NKJV), copyright 1982, 1988 by Thomas Nelson, Inc. used by permission. All rights reserved.

Scripture quotations marked (NASB) are from *Holy Bible, New American Standard* La Habra, CA: The Lockman Foundation, 1995.

Scripture quotations marked (ESV) are from *The Holy Bible, English Standard Version*, copyright ©2001 by Crossway Bibles, a publishing ministry of Good News Publishers. Used by permission. All rights reserved.

Scripture quotations marked (MLV) are from Modern Literal Version of The New Testament, Copyright 1999 by G. Allen Walker.

Scripture quotations marked (RSV) are from the Revised Standard Version of the Bible, copyright 1952 by the Division of Christian Education, National Council of the Churches of Christ in the United States of America.

Scripture quotations marked (NIV) are from the New International Version of the Holy Bible, copyright 1978 by Zondervan Bible publishers, Grand Rapids, Michigan.

Other Books by the Author

Topical Bible Studies

Growing a Godly Marriage & Raising Godly Children
Why Believe in God, Jesus, and the Bible? (evidences)
The God of the Bible (study of the Father, Son, and Holy Spirit)
Grace, Faith, and Obedience: The Gospel or Calvinism?
Kingdom of Christ: Future Millennium or Present Spiritual Reign?
Do Not Sin Against the Child: Abortion, Unborn Life, & the Bible
True Words of God: Bible Inspiration and Preservation

Commentaries on Bible Books

Genesis	*Gospel of Mark*
Joshua and Ruth	*Gospel of John*
Judges	*Acts*
1 Samuel	*Romans*
2 Samuel	*Galatians*
1 Kings	*Ephesians*
Ezra, Nehemiah, and Esther	*Philippians and Colossians*
Job	*Hebrews*
Proverbs	*James and Jude*
Ecclesiastes	*1 and 2 Peter*
Gospel of Matthew	*1,2,3 John*

Bible Question Class Books

Genesis	*Gospel of Matthew*
Joshua and Ruth	*Gospel of Mark*
Judges	*Gospel of Luke*
1 Samuel	*Gospel of John*
2 Samuel	*Acts*
1 Kings	*Romans*
Ezra, Nehemiah, and Esther	*1 Corinthians*
Job	*2 Corinthians and Galatians*
Proverbs	*Ephesians and Philippians*
Ecclesiastes	*Colossians, 1&2 Thessalonians*
Isaiah	*1 & 2 Timothy, Titus, Philemon*
Daniel	*Hebrews*
	General Epistles (James – Jude)
	Revelation

Workbooks with Study Notes

Jesus Is Lord: Workbook on the Fundamentals of the Gospel of Christ
Following Jesus: Workbook on Discipleship
God's Eternal Purpose in Christ: Workbook on the Theme of the Bible
Family Reading Booklist

**Visit our website at www.gospelway.com/sales to see a
current list of books in print.**

Study Notes on Joshua and Ruth

Other Resources from the Author

Printed books, booklets, and tracts available at
www.gospelway.com/sales
Free Bible study articles online at
www.gospelway.com
Free Bible courses online at
www.biblestudylessons.com
Free class books at
www.biblestudylessons.com/classbooks
Free commentaries on Bible books at
www.biblestudylessons.com/commentary
Contact the author at
www.gospelway.com/comments

Table of Contents

(Due to printer reformatting, the above numbers may be off a few pages.)

Study Notes on Joshua and Ruth

Notes to the Reader

To save space and for other reasons, I have chosen not to include the Bible text in these notes (please use your Bible to follow along). When I do quote a Scripture, I generally quote the New King James Version, unless otherwise indicated. Often – especially when I do not use quotations marks – I am not quoting any translation but simply paraphrasing the passage in my own words. Also, when I ask the reader to refer to a map, please consult the maps at the back of your Bible or in a Bible dictionary.

You can find study questions to accompany these notes at
www.gospelway.com/sales
To join our mailing list to be informed of new books or special sales, contact the author at
www.gospelway.com/comments

Introductory Thoughts about Commentaries

Only the Scriptures provide an infallible, authoritatively inspired revelation of God's will for man (2 Timothy 3:16,17). It follows that this commentary, like all commentaries, was written by an uninspired, fallible human. It is the author's effort to share his insights about God's word for the purpose of instructing and edifying others in the knowledge and wisdom found in Scripture. It is simply another form of teaching, like public preaching, Bible class teaching, etc., except in written form (like tracts, Bible class literature, etc.). Nehemiah 8:8; Ephesians 4:15,16; Romans 15:14; 1 Thessalonians 5:11; Hebrews 3:12-14; 5:12-14; 10:23-25; Romans 10:17; Mark 16:15,16; Acts 8:4; 2 Timothy 2:2,24-26; 4:2-4; 1 Peter 3:15.

It follows that the student must read any commentary with discernment, realizing that any fallible teacher may err, whether he is teaching orally or in writing. So, the student must compare all spiritual teaching to the truth of God's word (Acts 17:11). It may be wise to read several commentaries to consider alternative views on difficult points. But it is especially important to consider the *reasons or evidence* each author gives for his views, then compare them to the Bible.

For these reasons, the author urges the reader to always consider my comments in light of Scripture. Accept what I say only if you find that it harmonizes with God's word. And please do not cite my writings as authority, as though people should accept anything I say as authoritative. Always let the Bible be your authority.

"He who glories, let him glory in the Lord" – 1 Corinthians 1:31

Study Notes on Joshua and Ruth

Abbreviations Used in These Notes

ASV – American Standard Version
b/c/v – book, chapter, and verse
ESV – English Standard Version
f -– the following verse
ff – the following verses
KJV – King James Version
NASB – New American Standard Bible
NEB – New English Bible
NIV – New International Version
NKJV – New King James Version
RSV – Revised Standard Version
v – verse
vv – verses

Introduction to Joshua

Author

Joshua himself most likely wrote the historical record on which the book of Joshua is based (see 24:25-28). However, it is possible that some later inspired writer edited the account and added some material by inspiration of the Holy Spirit. Horne (see bibliography) discusses the possibilities at length.

Period of Bible History

Conquest of Canaan

Theme

God enables Israel to inherit the promised land of Canaan.

Main characters

Joshua, the Israelites

Background of Joshua's life:

* Led Israel in battle against Amalek (Exodus 17:9-14)
* Served as Moses' personal minister, accompanying him on Mt. Sinai (Exodus 24:13; 32:17; 33:11)
* Expressed jealousy that others prophesied besides Moses (Numbers 11:28)
* Sent into Canaan as one of 12 spies. Only he and Caleb said Israel could conquer Canaan, so only those two were allowed to enter (Numbers 13&14; 26:65; 32:12).
* Appointed as Moses' successor as leader of the nation (Numbers 27:15-23; Deuteronomy 31:7,8; 34:9).

Notice that Joshua was trained to prepare him to take the place of Moses as the leader of the people. This was done by experience and especially by working with Moses to learn from him principles of good leadership. This is an important Biblical principle. God's people need to train those who can serve in leadership roles.

In particular, people need to learn to serve by working with those who are more experienced. Jesus trained the apostles by taking them with Him throughout His public ministry so they could learn from Him how to be effective teachers. The apostle Paul always had other men with him on his preaching trips, including young men such as Timothy and Mark. Likewise today, those who are older and more experienced in teaching and leading among God's people need to train those who are younger or more experienced by taking them along in their teaching work so they can learn by observing and then by experience.

"Joshua" (Hebrew) means Jehovah Savior and is equivalent to Greek "Jesus." Just as Joshua provided salvation for the nation of Israel by leading them into the promised land of Canaan, so Jesus Christ provides salvation for all mankind by offering us eternal life in the promised land of heaven.

Introductory notes

Note the relationship between this book and God's promise to Abraham.

God had promised three major blessings to Abraham's descendants: 1) a great nation, 2) possession of Canaan, and 3) a blessing on all nations (salvation through Jesus) to come on all nations through His descendants -- Gen. 12:2,3,7; 15:5-8,18-21; 13:15,17; 18:18; 22:17,18; 24:7; 26:3,4,24; 28:3,4; 32:12.

Israel had become a great nation while in Egyptian captivity, fulfilling the first promise. By God's mercy, Moses had led them out of Egypt and given them the law. He led them to Canaan the first time they approached the land, but they refused to enter. God punished them by making them wander forty years in the wilderness. Moses led them through that wandering; but because he himself later sinned, he was not allowed to enter the land.

Moses led the people to capture the land east of Jordan, and divided it between the tribes of Reuben, Gad, and half of Manasseh. He died in sight of the land west of Jordan, and Joshua was appointed to lead the people into the land.

This book reveals the fulfillment of the second promise to Abraham – the land promise. Note 11:23; 21:43-45; 23:14. As such, Joshua is a symbol of Jesus, who leads us to the eternal promised land (Heb. 4:5-16).

Facts about the land of Canaan (see a map)

The following is a summary of information from the Waldron's notes:

Canaan is bounded by the Mediterranean Sea on the west and on the east the Jordan River, the Sea of Galilee, and the Dead Sea (although the 2½ tribes did inherit territory east of Jordan). From north to south it stretches from mountainous regions north of the Sea of Galilee to the desert area south of the Dead Sea.

Dan was generally considered the northernmost city and Beersheeba the southernmost, a distance of 150 miles between them. East to west the area is about 30 miles across in the north and 55 miles in the south. The whole territory is smaller than almost every individual state of the USA.

When Israel inherited the land, it was very fertile and productive as indicated by the fruit found there by the 12 spies. However, due to the people's unfaithfulness, God later brought curses on the land as He had promised to do; as a result, today it is generally dry and unproductive.

The main bodies of water are the Mediterranean Sea, the Jordan River, the Sea of Galilee, and the Dead Sea.

Near the Sea on the west is a coastal plain. This plain is the area of Phoenicia north of Mt. Carmel. South of that mountain for a ways is the Plain of Sharon. The area south of that is Philistia.

Between this coastal plain and the Jordan valley is the Hill Country, a ridge of mountains running almost the length of the country. The Jordan valley separates these mountains from a plateau east of Jordan that stretches to the Arabian Desert.

This is the territory that God had promised to give Israel. However, He said that keeping the land and prospering in it would depend on their faithfulness to Him. As a result, they actually held more or less of the land at various times.

Peoples of the land

God named the peoples of the land that He promised to give the Israelites as follows: Canaanites, Amorites, Hittites, Girgashites, Perizzites, Hivites, and Jebusites (Exodus 3:17; Deut. 7:1; etc.). These were really tribes living in different areas of the land. The strongest of them were the Amorites, Canaanites, and Hittites. Most of these tribes inhabited the land west of Jordan. But the Amorites lived predominately just east of Jordan.

Still further east from the Amorites lived the Ammonites. South of the Armorites lived the Moabites and then the Edomites. These peoples were distant relatives of Israel as descendants of Lot and Esau. God commanded Israel to seek to be peaceable with these nations and did not promise to give their lands to Israel (though they often attacked Israel resulting in war).

These are the lands and the peoples we will discuss at some length in the book of Joshua as Israel fought against them to take their lands in fulfillment of God's promise.

God commanded Israel, not just to take the lands of these people, but to utterly destroy the people and their idols. They were to make no marriages with these people. Otherwise, the nations would influence Israel to commit idolatry with their gods (Deut. 7; 9:1-6). We will see that Israel fulfilled this command only partially, resulting in exactly the problems God predicted.

Outline of the book

A. Israel Enters Canaan (Joshua 1-5)

* Joshua appointed to replace Moses to lead Israel into Canaan – Num. 27:18-23; 34:17; Deut. 1:38; 3:21,28; 31:3,7,14,23; 34:9; Josh. 1

* Two spies sent into Jericho spared from capture by Rahab (Josh. 2)

* Israel allowed to miraculously cross the Jordan River on dry ground; memorial of 12 stones (Josh. 3&4; note 3:14-17; 4:1-9)

* Circumcision of males (chapter 5)

B. Israel Conquers Canaan (Joshua 6-12)

* Conquest of Jericho – (Josh. 6; note 6:1-5,20-23)
* Sin of Achan & defeat of Ai (Josh. 7&8; note 7:16-26)
* Alliance with Gibeonites (Josh. 9)
* Southern conquest; sun standing still (Josh. 10; note 10:9-13)
* Northern conquest (Josh. 11)

C. Israel Divides Canaan (Joshua 13-24)

* Division of the land among the tribes (Josh. 13-22), including appointing the cities of refuge (chapter 20)

* Joshua's final discourses (Josh. 23,24)

Part 1. Israel Enters Canaan – Joshua 1-5

Joshua 1

Joshua Appointed to Lead the People – Joshua 1

1:1-9 - Command to Joshua to Lead the People

1:1-4 – God commanded Joshua to lead the people in the place of Moses. He would give the people all the land that He had promised.

Before Moses died, Joshua had been appointed by God to take Moses' place (see Introduction). After Moses died, God spoke to Joshua and gave him the charge to lead Israel into the land. He promised the whole land to Israel, just as it had been promised to Moses and as far back as Abraham.

The area is here described as extending from the wilderness and Lebanon to the Euphrates River, including all the land of the Hittites, then to the Great Sea (Mediterranean) on the west. Joshua may, at this time, have been standing on an elevated place viewing the land as Moses had done before he died. Lebanon was the area along the Mediterranean directly north of Israel. The Euphrates was further north but to the east from there.

The Hittites lived throughout much of this region. Of the nations who lived in the area, sometimes one or the other is named specifically as though referring to the whole area. Perhaps the Hittites were the dominant tribe at that time west of Jordan. Or perhaps they just stood as representative of all the tribes.

In any case, God promised clearly that Israel would eventually control all this territory. They did not control this full extent in Joshua's lifetime. Only in the kingdoms of David and Solomon did Israel control the full extent of territory God predicted.

Joseph Free points out that the Bible contains some 40 references to the Hittites. Nevertheless, for many years a number of scholars doubted or denied the existence of such a people. Free describes how archaeology settled the issue:

> Discoveries during the twentieth century, however, left no doubt concerning the Hittites. In 1906, Hugo Winckler of Berlin went to the site known as Boghaz-koi, in central Turkey, and there examined the remains of what proved to be the capital of the Hittite Empire. He found an archive of clay tablets ..., which contained, among many other documents, a military treaty made between the Hittites and the Egyptians nearly 1300 years before the time of Christ.

Today there is no doubt about the existence of the Hittites. In fact, I understand that whole museums have been devoted to their history.

1:5-9 – Joshua should be strong and of good courage to observe all the law revealed by Moses, because God would be with him wherever he went.

God promised that He would be with Joshua as He had been with Moses. He would not leave nor forsake him. The result would be that no one would be able to stand before Joshua throughout his whole life – i.e., no one could withstand or successfully oppose him in the work he did for the Lord.

Because of God's protection and provision, Joshua would succeed in bringing Israel into the promised land. God gave him this task and assured him it could be done. This would fulfill the promise to Abraham and the fathers to give this land to them (see Introduction).

However, the promise was conditional. There were things Joshua would need to do to be successful. Remember, Israel had attempted to do this once before but failed because of *fear* (Num. 13:31,33; 14:6-9). So three times God told Joshua to "*be strong and of good courage*" (verses 6,7,9).

We too face hardship in serving God.

God's people have always had great responsibilities to work for Him. We do not have the same challenges or charge that God gave Joshua. But we do have a charge from God and we will face challenges. We get discouraged and fearful, thinking we cannot succeed. Nothing should be of greater encouragement, when we face these responsibilities, than the assurance that God will help us accomplish them.

Luke 6:22,23; Psalms 27:1-3,14 – We face persecution and opposition from evildoers.

Psalms 46:1,2; 23:4 -- We face tasks of obedience and service that we must accomplish for the Lord. Often we face hardships and difficulties in accomplishing this work: illness, death, family problems, financial hardship, temptation to sin, etc. It takes great courage to face these and continue serving God. (John 14:27; Psa. 49:5; 91:5ff; 112:7,8; Heb. 11:23)

Ephesians 6:19,20; Acts 4:10-13,18-20,29-31 – We are responsible to teach others the gospel. Many people will oppose these efforts. (Acts 13:46; 9:27,29; 14:3; 18:26; 19:8; 18:9; 1 Thess. 2:2,4; Gal. 2:12; Phil. 1:14)

As with Joshua, we need encouragement and assurance that we too can succeed in God's work. God gave Joshua three things to help him be successful. These same things give us success in our duties in God's service.

God gave a goal, and assured Joshua he could reach it – verses 6,8.

The goal was to lead the people into the land. God promised Joshua he could definitely achieve this goal. Hope of success in achieving a great goal gives great motivation to be strong and courageous.

Revelation 2:10 – Do not fear persecution, but be faithful till death and you'll receive a crown of life. So a great goal can produce great courage.

Hebrews 11:32-38 – God's people in the Old Testament showed great courage. Why? Verse 16 – They looked for a better country.

Just as Joshua was brave to lead the people into the promised land, so God has offered us the promised land of eternal life, and He has assured us we can successfully reach it. This ought to make us strong and brave.

[2 Chron. 15:7,8; Matt. 10:32,33; Rev.21:8; 2 Cor. 5:6,8; Isa. 35:2-4]

Study Notes on Joshua and Ruth

God gave guidance and instruction – verses 7-9.

God instructed Joshua what to do and how to do it. He told him to observe the law as revealed by Moses, study it diligently and obey it without moving away from it to the right or to the left. How would this also give us courage and lead to success? Everyone needs wisdom in order to reach a goal successfully. It is much easier to be brave when you have received proper guidance and instruction.

Jeremiah 1:7-9 – Jeremiah was afraid to speak for God. God said to be not afraid because he would be speaking God's word. When we know what God's will is, and we really trust that He is always right, this gives us courage and guides us to success.

We often speak of people who act out of the "courage of their convictions." It is hard to act courageously when we're not sure what is the right thing to do. So, if we know what God has commanded us to do, and we really believe His way is best, this makes us strong and courageous. We are much more likely to be successful.

It follows that sometimes people fail in God's work because of lack of study. If we have the commands, but we don't know what they say, of course we will not succeed.

When we reject God's way, or don't know God's way, sooner or later the result will be fear and failure. If we want courage and success in serving God, we must study His word and be convicted it is best.

[Prov. 1:25-33; 3:19-26; 1 Chron. 22:13; Josh. 23:6-10]

God promised to be with Joshua – verses 5,9.

It is much easier to be brave and successful when you have someone strong and wise on your side to help you. Just as God promised to be with Joshua in his physical battles, so He has promised to be with us in our spiritual battles.

Romans 8:31 – If God is for us, who can be against us?

Psalms 23:4 – Yea, though I walk through the valley of the shadow of death, I will fear no evil; For You are with me.

1 Samuel 17:9-11 – Goliath, a ten-foot-tall giant challenged Israel to fight, and all Israel was afraid. But David fought him without armor, only a sling and stones. Where did David get the courage? How did he succeed? Verses 36,45,47 – God was on David's side. The battle was the Lord's.

2 Chronicles 32:7,8 – When Assyria besieged Jerusalem, Hezekiah encouraged the people to be strong and of good courage, because God was with them. Why did God's presence give strength? Because of His **power**. All the enemy had was the arm of flesh, but we have Jehovah to help fight for us.

It follows that people often fail in God's work, because we lack faith in God.

Matthew 14:25,28-31 – Jesus came to His apostles walking on the water. Peter began walking to Jesus, but became afraid and began to sink. Why? Lack of faith. Jesus was with him, but he looked at the waves instead of at Jesus. So, we lose courage and fail when we look at how great our problems are and take our eyes off how great our God is.

2 Kings 6:14-17 – The Syrian army surrounded Elisha, and his servant was afraid. Elisha said to fear not, because he had more on his side than the enemy did on theirs. The servant's eyes were opened and he saw the mountain full of horses and fiery chariots protecting Elisha.

Joshua could be brave and successful in God's work if he kept his eye on the goal, studied and followed God's word diligently, and trusted in God to be with him. We can succeed in our work for God in the same way.

[Psa. 31:13-15; Matt. 8:23ff; 2 Chron. 15:1-8; Psa. 27:11-14; 31:23f; 46:1,2; Isa. 41:10-13; 43:1-5; Heb. 13:5,6; Josh 23:6-10]

1:10-18 - Preparation to Cross the River

1:10,11 – Joshua commanded the officers to prepare the people to cross the Jordan within three days.

Having received instructions and encouragement from the Lord, Joshua began to prepare the people to cross the Jordan into Canaan.

He commanded the officers to instruct the people in the camp to prepare provisions (food) and be ready in three days to cross the Jordan and go in to possess the land.

1:12-15 – Joshua reminded the tribes that would settle east of the Jordan that they must go with the rest of Israel to capture the land west of the Jordan.

Two and one half tribes had received their inheritance already on the east side of Jordan. When Israel had conquered this land, these tribes had found it such good land for raising flocks that they asked to receive their inheritance there.

Moses had agreed on condition that they must agree to leave their families behind and go into Canaan with the other tribes when they went to fight to take the land. After the other tribes had taken their lands, then the 2½ tribes could return to their families and live in the land they had received.

Study Notes on Joshua and Ruth

It would not have been fair for all the tribes to fight for the land these tribes received, if they had then refused to fight to help the other tribes take their territories. The 2½ tribes had agreed to this arrangement. See Numbers 32. Here Joshua reminds them of this agreement.

Notice that when they received the land and possessed it, Joshua referred to this as being given rest – verses 13-15. This is used as a symbol of our eternal rest of heaven in Hebrews 4:1-11.

1:16-18 – The people promised to obey Joshua even as they had obeyed Moses. Anyone who rebelled should be put to death.

Not only did the 2½ tribes agree to keep their word and go into the land to help the other tribes capture it, but they also gave their promise of allegiance to Joshua. They promised to do as he commanded and go where he would send them. (Note: It is clear that the people who made this promise included the 2½ tribes. It is likely that all the other tribes joined in the promise as well.)

They promised that they would follow Joshua just as they had followed Moses. They expressed their desire for God to be with him as He had been with Moses. And they said anyone who would not follow but rebelled against him would be put to death. In this they encouraged him to be strong even as God had encouraged him.

No doubt this was well intended. However, assurance that they would follow Joshua as they had followed Moses would not give much reassurance. They had not done a very good job of following Moses at times. They had followed him in the battles to capture the area east of Jordan. But they had rebelled time and again throughout their history.

In any case, they clearly here meant to give assurance to Joshua of their intent to fully follow and obey him. This was a good start. If such determination could continue, they would have had a successful labor for the Lord.

Joshua 2

Two Spies Sent into Jericho – Joshua 2

2:1-11 - The Spies Hidden by Rahab

2:1-3 – When Rahab received the two men sent to spy out Jericho, the king charged her to deliver them up.

Joshua had encamped the people in a place here called Acacia Grove (compare 3:1; Num. 25:1). Before sending the army into the land, Joshua determined to send spies to view the land. This was reminiscent of his own duty as a spy when Moses sent the twelve spies the first time Israel approached to take the land.

The first significant city they were to confront was Jericho, so that is where Joshua sent the spies. (See **map**.)

Rahab the harlot receives the spies

The spies went into the city and there were received by a woman named Rahab who was a harlot or prostitute. Some claim the Hebrew word does not necessarily mean a prostitute, but the Greek words in the references in Hebrews and James surely confirm that she was a prostitute. She had been a wicked woman, but she here demonstrated faith in God. Some commentators wonder if perhaps she had forsaken her life of immorality even before the events in this chapter, but is still referred to as a harlot on the basis of her past life. For her faith she is mentioned elsewhere as an example for us. See Heb. 11:31; James 2:25.

We are not told how the spies found her nor what about her background may have led her to have a heart different from others in Jericho. The Waldrons suggest that the spies knew they would be recognized as foreigners, so they may have deliberately chosen to

Study Notes on Joshua and Ruth

visit a harlot, thinking the people would believe they were there for immoral purposes rather than as spies.

In any case, she received the spies into her home. But the king of the city heard that Israel had sent spies into the city, and apparently he knew that Rahab had received them. He sent messengers to her to tell him where the men were, since they were spies sent to view the land.

Interestingly, Matthew 1:5 lists a Rahab in the lineage of Jesus. However, Young's concordance lists this as a different woman than this harlot in Jericho. The Rahab in Jesus' lineage was the mother of the Boaz who later married Ruth, great grandmother of King David. That would perhaps have put the Rahab in Matthew's account later in history than the Rahab here in Joshua 2. However, one wonders why that Rahab is mentioned in Jesus' lineage, when the only other women named were Tamar, Ruth, and Mary (Bathsheeba is also mentioned but not named).

2:4-7 – Rahab said the men had left by the gate, but really she had hidden them on her roof.

Rahab admitted to the king that the men had come to her, but she said she had no knowledge of where they were from. She said they left in the dark as the gate was being shut. So she did not know where they had gone, but the king's men might overtake them if they quickly pursued them.

However, this was not just deception but was an outright lie. She did know where they were from and she knew they had not left at all. In fact, they were still on her roof where she had hidden them among some stalks of flax on her roof (v6).

Acting on this misinformation, the king's men went by way of the road to the Jordan, hoping to overtake the spies. As soon as the pursuers had gone, the gate was shut, presumably as a safety precaution.

Was Rahab's lie justified?

While Rahab had come to believe in God, she apparently was still willing to violate a basic command of God's law. She clearly told a lie. Yet God later identifies her by name as a woman who acted by faith and was blessed for her faith – Heb. 11:31; James 2:25. How can her conduct be justified?

There are only two possible explanations I can think of: Either (1) Lying was justified when necessary to save life (as in wartime), or (2) Her lie was not justified but God saved her for her faith despite her lie.

Note that she is not commended in either of the New Testament passages for having told a lie. Hebrews 11:31 commends her for her faith in receiving the spies in peace. James 2:25 commends her for her faith in receiving the spies and sending them out another way (so they could avoid their enemies). Neither one says her lie was justified, nor do they say that the lie was an act of faith.

Remember that she had been a wicked woman, who had only recently come to believe in the true God. She might not yet know lying was a violation of the law of her new God, yet she was rewarded for her faith in hiding the spies and sending them away safely. This would require great faith, and for that God commended and rewarded her, not for her lie. Remember, other great servants of God also committed sins. They are not rewarded for their sins but for their acts of faith. Rahab had been a prostitute too and that is even mentioned in the New Testament references to her faith. Is that here justified? Not at all. To truly please God, she must repent of that and learn to do better. Why not say the same of her lie?

And even if her act may have been justified under the Old Testament, that would not prove it would be justified today. The Old Testament allowed many acts of war not allowed today.

2:8-11 – Rahab explained that she knew God had given the land to Israel, and the inhabitants were fainthearted because they heard what God had done.

Rahab went up on her roof that night, before the spies went to sleep, and explained to them why she had helped them. She said she knew that God had given the land to the Israelites, and that the people of the land were in mortal terror of the Israelites.

The people had heard about God's dealings with Israel in leading them across the Red Sea on dry land and leading them to victory over the kingdoms of Sihon and Og on the east side of Jordan. She explained that hearing these things had caused the hearts of the people of Jericho to melt in fear. They had no courage left. As a result, she was convinced that the God of heaven and earth was with Israel. See Deuteronomy 11:25.

This demonstrates the purpose of miracles, such as the crossing of the Red Sea. They occurred to give people evidence to believe in God's existence and that certain people were from Him. The military victories confirmed His power to defeat Israel's enemies.

The ultimate goal of all these events was that God might gain honor. As a result, the people would fear the Lord and believe in Him – Exodus 14:14-18,21-31. Rahab's affirmation that the people of Jericho had heard of these great miracles demonstrates that God

Study Notes on Joshua and Ruth

had truly accomplished His purpose. People even as far away as Canaan had heard of the plagues upon Egypt and the crossing of the Red Sea. This had caused their hearts to melt and to fear God and the people of Israel.

This explains why Rahab had acted as she did: she had come to believe in the God of Israel as the true God. Other people, of course, had heard the same stories, but they did not believe as she did. No doubt these people worshipped many gods and had simply been convinced that this was a very powerful god. Yet most of them were still not willing to work on behalf of Israel against their own people. Rahab's faith was unusual and God rewarded her for it.

2:12-24 - The Spies' Agreement with Rahab

2:12-14 – Rahab requested that all her family be spared when Israel conquered the city.

Having explained why she believed in God's intent to bless Israel, Rahab offered an agreement with the spies. Since she had shown them kindness, she asked them to show her kindness and spare her family (father, mother, brothers, and sisters) and all they had from death. She asked them to swear and give a token of this agreement.

The men agreed to spare her life for theirs if she would not tell others about their purpose in being in the city. If so, they promised God would deal kindly with her when He had given them the land.

This raises another issue. God had commanded Israel to slay all the inhabitants of the land (see introductory notes on the people of the land). Yet here the spies were agreeing to do otherwise before the people even attempted to enter. This would appear to be justified in this case, however, on grounds of the reason God gave for the command. He had said to slay the people else they would lead Israel into idolatry. In this case, however, Rahab had become a believer. Later such people would be called proselytes. Proselytes, in effect, became Jews by conversion. Presumably, such believers should have been spared, not killed. In that case, the spies' agreement was justified.

2:15,16 – Rahab let the spies escape over the wall and told them to hide three days on the mountain.

Rahab's house was on the wall of the city with a window looking over or through the wall. So they would not have to go out through the city gate that would be guarded, she let them out through the window and down the wall by a rope.

She told them to go to the mountains to escape and hide there three days. The pursuers had gone toward the Jordan. By going the other way, the spies could hide in the mountains and then, when the pursuers had given up, they could cross the Jordan to Israel.

2:17-21 – The spies agreed to save all Rahab's family if they would be in her house with a scarlet cord in the window and she would not betray the spies.

The spies first gave her a sign and made clear the conditions she must meet to be spared. First, she must tie a scarlet cord in the window through which they had escaped. Then she must be sure everyone who would be saved was in her house. They would not guarantee the safety of anyone outside the house, but they would be responsible if anyone in the house was killed. And third, she must not tell anyone about their business in being there. If she did not keep these conditions, they would be free from their oath to her. Rahab agreed and sent them away.

Note that, in order for people besides Rahab to be saved, they too would almost surely need faith. Why would they agree to be in the house on the wall when Israel attacked, unless they were convinced they could be saved there?

Rahab as an illustration of our salvation

This story is used to illustrate our salvation in Hebrews 11:31 and James 2:25. So consider some lessons we can learn.

(1) We too must have faith to be saved (see the context of both Heb. 11 and James 2).

(2) Our faith also must show itself by meeting conditions – we are saved by faith that works, not by faith only – see James 2:25 in context. The conditions faith requires of us include baptism (Mark 16:15,16; Acts 2:38; 22:16; Romans 6:3,4; Galatians 3:27; 1 Peter 3:21). Those who argue for salvation by faith alone need to reckon with the illustration of Rahab.

In particular, notice how Rahab here demonstrated great faith by her conduct. She did not simply wish the spies well while saying there was nothing she could do to help them because of the danger of being detected and punished by the people of Jericho. She risked her life to save them because of her faith that the God they worshiped was the true God and would surely give victory to Israel.

She not only hid the men, she advised them specific steps to take to escape detection. Then she made an agreement with them to spare her life and the lives of her family when Israel conquered the city. Had she not been certain that God would give them victory, she may have reasoned that she should not help them because, if they failed to capture the city, she could be put to death for treason. She is held up as an example of the kind of faith we need to be saved, because she risked all in expression of her faith in the true God.

Henry points out that Rahab had only heard about the works of God in the nation of Israel. Yet she demonstrated greater faith than many people in the nation of Israel who had been eyewitnesses of those very acts.

(3) Specifically, faith often requires that people be in a certain place or relationship in order to be saved. Rahab's family had to be in the house to be saved. We must be in the church to be saved. The church in the New Testament refers to the body of all saved people (Acts 2:47; 20:28; Eph. 5:23,25). The house did not save Rahab's family, but they had to be there to be among the saved. Likewise, the church does not save us, but we must be there to be among the saved.

2:22-24 – The spies escaped and reported to Joshua that God had delivered the land into their hands and the inhabitants were fainthearted because of Israel.

As Rahab had advised, the spies fled to the mountains and stayed there three days till the pursuers had returned. Then they left the mountains, crossed the Jordan, and reported to Joshua all that had happened.

Their conclusion, based on what they had seen and no doubt especially on what Rahab had told them, was that the people of the land were fearful and fainthearted. Surely God would deliver the land to the Israelites. Note how their report differed from that of the ten spies the first time Israel had approached the land.

Joshua 3

Israel Crosses the Jordan River – Joshua 3,4

Joshua 3 - The Crossing on Dry Ground

3:1-4 – At the Jordan Joshua said the priests should carry the ark of the covenant and the people should follow.

Having received the spies' report, the people left their camp early in the morning and approached the Jordan. Before crossing it, however, they camped there a while. After three days, the officers gave the people their instructions (this could be three days after they had left camp or perhaps three days after some other event – this is not clear to me).

The people were instructed to follow the Ark of the Covenant. The priests and Levites would bear the ark, as God had commanded them to do (Numbers 4:15; Exodus 25:14). But in this case the ark would go before the people and they would follow it, with a space of 2000 cubits (3000 feet – over half a mile) between the ark and the people. The only explanation for this arrangement was that this would show them what way to travel. The people would not know what way to travel otherwise, since they had never passed that way before.

Of course, the whole way was new to them, so they would not know the way to travel without guidance. But God could have chosen some other way to guide them. In particular, there would have been no obvious reason for such a large space between the people and the ark. God chose this way by His Divine wisdom, and the people would obey if they trusted Him. As the story shows, the ark was to pass first into the river and cause it to dry up so the

Study Notes on Joshua and Ruth

people could pass on dry land. Perhaps this is why God wanted such a large space of separation between it and the people.

In a similar sense, we all need God's guidance every day of our lives. Each of us has one and only one life in which to live to please God and receive His blessing of eternal life. If we wish to pass successfully, we too need to follow His guidance, for we have never passed through life before. He guides us through His word. We may think we know better than what His word says, or we may think we don't need His word but can go on our own. Then we get into trouble. If we trust Him, we will realize that He is the only One who really knows what life is about and the best way to live it. So we will obey His will in faith.

[Matthew 15:9,13; Galatians 1:8,9; 2 John 9-11; Colossians 3:17; Jeremiah 10:23; Proverbs 14:12; 3:5,6; Revelation 22:18,19; 1 Timothy 1:3; 2 Timothy 1:13]

3:5-8 – *The priests who bore the ark of the covenant should stand in the water at the edge of the Jordan.*

Joshua then instructed the people to sanctify themselves, since God would do wonders (miracles) among them. To sanctify is to make holy or set apart. This was done in various ways, depending on God's specific commands. This account does not tell us exactly what was involved in this case, so we do not know the specifics. It may have involved simply dedication of heart or attitude, or it may have involved other specifics simply not listed here. (See 7:13; Ex. 19:10,11.)

Joshua then instructed the priests who carried the ark to begin the march. They were to precede the people, as just described in verses 3,4, so they were to take up the ark and begin.

The Lord instructed Joshua (at that moment or earlier) that God was going to do a miracle. As with all miracles this would confirm that God was working through a man of His choosing, so the people would know to believe the words of that man. (See Mark 16:20; John 5:36; 20:30,31; Acts 2:22; 14:3; 2 Corinthians 12:11,12; Hebrews 2:3,4; 1 Kings 18:36-39; Exodus 4:1-9; 7:3-5; 14:30,31.)

God had already called Joshua to take Moses' place as leader and the people had promised to follow him (chapter 1). But great faith would be required of the people and of Joshua. The previous generation had approached the land before and had turned back due to lack of faith. So God here gave miraculous confirmation so the people would have faith to know God was working through Joshua as He had worked through Moses.

The miracle God had planned would require the priests bearing the ark to walk into the waters of the Jordan and stand there. Further instructions will follow in the next verses.

This would especially take faith because, as we will see later, the Jordan was at flood stage at this time. Walking out into a river of any size at any time would take some faith, but especially when it was flooding. Near the city of Jericho, the Jordan is about to enter the Dead Sea. It is at its largest size of any point. Crossing it here at flood stage would be especially dangerous and difficult. Perhaps the inhabitants thought the army of Israel could not cross at all at that time. In any case, Joshua told the priests to have the faith to carry the ark into the river.

3:9-13 – Joshua said that the water of the Jordan would be cut off when the feet of the priests bearing the ark rested in the waters.

Joshua then called the people together and described the miracle that God was about to perform. He said that it would confirm to the people that God would keep His promise to give them the land. Miracles not only served to confirm that God was working through a specific inspired man, but they also gave the people evidence to believe in God Himself. They should know that He is the true God and they should follow Him in faith. Note that He is here called the Lord of all the earth. He was not just the Lord of one nation or one part of the world, but the Lord of the whole earth.

Joshua said that the priests would carry the ark before them (as described above – verses 3,4,6) and would cross the Jordan before the people. But when the feet of the priests carrying the ark stood in the river, God would cause the water to be stopped upstream from them. The river would be blocked, so the water would stand up in a heap and would cease to flow downstream.

We are not told what would block the river, but clearly it would be an act of God. And it was surely a miracle in that Joshua knew ahead of time that it would happen and when it would happen. It would happen at the very time that the priests would walk into the river. Perhaps it was also miraculous in that the water may have been held in a way that was impossible by natural means, as the Red Sea had been held when Israel had crossed it. But in any case, the fact that it happened when Joshua said so would prove that God was working through Joshua. Note the crossing of the Jordan was a sign that Joshua was God's appointed leader just as the crossing of the Red Sea had been a sign the Moses was God's appointed leader.

Study Notes on Joshua and Ruth

Joshua also told each of the twelve tribes to appoint a man for a special job. We are not here told what that job was, but it will be revealed in the next chapter. As Israel crossed the river, these twelve men would have a special job to do.

3:14-17 – When the priests carrying the ark stepped into the Jordan, the waters were cut off so all the people were able to cross on dry ground.

So as Joshua commanded, the people began to march as led by the priests. When the priests carrying the ark stepped into the river, the waters rose in a heap upstream at a town named Adam, near Zaretan. The water flowing toward the Salt or Dead Sea was cut off, and the people crossed the river on dry ground across from Jericho.

The priests then stood with the ark in the middle of the riverbed until all the people crossed. As long as they stayed in the river, the water continued to be held back so the people could cross.

Verse 15 tells us, as mentioned in previous notes, that this happened at the time of harvest when Jordan was at flood stage. This miracle may have been hard enough any time, but especially so when the river was flooded.

This would also take faith on the part of the people to cross the river. They might wonder if, at any moment, the water would start to come again with them in the middle of the river. They needed faith that God would allow them to cross safely.

The miracle that resulted thereby confirmed God's power and the people's faith in Him. He had done a miracle to allow them to cross the river. It would also confirm the people's faith in Joshua as God's spokesman, since the miracle had occurred at his word. See Psalm 114:1-8.

And finally, the miracle would no doubt become known to the people of Jericho and the other people of the land. In fact, the whole nation of Israel crossed the Jordan River miraculously at one of the nearest locations to Jericho – verse 16. Such a bold move would give the people of Jericho ample opportunity to know about the miracle. This would cause them to further fear Israel and her God even more than they were already frightened. They had already heard of the crossing of the Red Sea (2:10). Knowing that Israel had likewise miraculously crossed the Jordan to enter their own land would further demoralize the Canaanites.

Joshua 4

Joshua 4 - The Memorial Stones

4:1-3 – One man from each of the twelve tribes should take a stone from the middle of the river where the feet of the priests had stood.

When all the people had crossed the Jordan safely, God spoke to Joshua with instructions about the memorials they were to make. Twelve men were chosen, one from each tribe. Actually, these are almost surely the men Joshua had already mentioned in 3:12. Here God gave instructions what the men were to do.

These men were to go to the place in the river where the feet of the priests stood. There each man was to take a stone from the riverbed and carry it to the place where Israel would camp that night.

Later instructions would tell what purpose the stones would serve. But at this point it is important that these stones came from the very riverbed itself. Clearly it would be hard or impossible to obtain them normally. But with the river dried up by God's power, it was easy to obtain them.

4:4-7 – The stones taken from the middle of the river would be set up as a memorial for future generations.

Joshua then told each of the twelve men to carry his stone on his shoulder and cross to the west side of the river ahead of the priests with the ark. The water remained held back so long as the priests and the ark stayed in the river, so the men had to get the stones and carry them to land before the priests left the river.

The stones would be a memorial sign to future generations to remember the crossing of the river. When future generations asked about the stones, the people would explain how the waters of the river were cut off so the ark (and the people) were enabled to cross over on dry ground. The stones would be a memorial to the people forever.

Study Notes on Joshua and Ruth

Note that God wants people to remember His great acts, and He has often authorized memorials whereby we can remember them. People tend to forget what God has done, if they are not reminded. Especially God's miracles were done to convince the people to believe in God. Future generations would not see the miracle, but the stones would remind them and would remind the parents to teach the children. We too need to remember to teach our children about God's great works of the past.

Note the use of the word "forever." This illustrates that this Old Testament word simply means for a long indefinite period of time. Are the stones still there? Not likely. And if they were, they would be so worn away we could not tell which stones they were, so they could not serve the desired purpose for us. "Forever" in the Old Testament does not mean a thing that never ends even into all eternity.

Observations about memorials

Memorials in the Old Testament often consisted of stones or piles of stones. See Exodus 20; Genesis 31:43-53; Joshua 24:25-27; 1 Samuel 7:11,12. The 10 Commands were written on stones as a memorial to God's law. They were not the whole law, nor even necessarily the most important laws. They were a visible memorial to remind people of the law.

God's memorials today under the New Testament include the Lord's Supper, which is a memorial feast reminding us of Jesus' death. Also, the Bible is a written book reminding us, not just of God's law, but of His great miracles. We cannot see miracles today, even as Israel could not continue to see the Jordan dried up. But we have the memorial of them in the Bible (John 20:30,31).

4:8,9 – Joshua also set up twelve stones in the middle of the river where the feet of the priests had stood.

The men did as Joshua commanded. Each of them took a stone from the midst of Jordan and carried it to the camp. There they laid them down, probably in a pile or heap.

But Joshua set up a second memorial. This one also consisted of twelve stones, but it was set up in the midst of the Jordan River. This was also in the place where the priests had stood while holding the ark.

This cannot be the same pile of stones that the twelve men took from the riverbed. Those stones were removed from the riverbed and placed on the ground in the camp as a memorial. These stones Joshua set up (v9) were stones still in the riverbed.

This would serve as a further confirmation that God had held back the river. How could one make a pile of stones in the middle of a river? It would again normally be difficult or impossible in that day. But it was easy while the river was dried up.

The writer comments that, whenever the book was written (probably near the time of Joshua's death) the pile of stones was still there. No doubt the river eventually wore them away, but they would have stood for many generations as a testimony to God's miracle.

So the people had two stone memorials of this event. One pile on land consisted of stones that had been removed from the river. The other pile consisted of stones piled up in the midst of the river. Both memorials served the same purpose.

(A few looser translations describe just one stone memorial, but all the more conservative ones describe two.)

4:10,11 – When all the people had crossed, then the priests carrying the ark also left the river.

The priests continued standing in the midst of the river, holding that ark as long as it was necessary for the water to be held back. Everything God had commanded had to be finished before they came out of the water. So the people hurried across, the stone memorials were accomplished as needed. And the priests had to stay in the riverbed the whole time.

4:12-14 – The men of the 2½ tribes led the people into the land.

The men of the tribes that settled east of Jordan had promised to go with Israel into the land (see on 1:12-18). Joshua had reminded them of this commitment, and they fulfilled it. They were apparently the first to cross over into the new land.

About 40,000 men of war crossed before God to the plains of Jericho prepared for battle. Based on the numbers of men counted in Numbers 26, this must have been the count of the men from the 2½ tribes. There were far more men than this even in those tribes, let alone all the tribes combined. The census counted all men age 20 and up, but doubtless many of them were not able to serve as soldiers. So presumably this was the number from the 2½ tribes who were able to fight.

The miracle the people saw at the river served to exalt Joshua in the sight of the people. They realized he was truly from God, so they listened to him as they had Moses before him. This was the purpose of miracles. See on 3:7.

Study Notes on Joshua and Ruth

4:15-18 – When the priests carrying the ark left the river, the water returned to its normal place.

The priests had to stay in the riverbed until everyone had crossed and nothing more needed to be done in the river. This was all accomplished now, so God gave the command to Joshua to tell the priests to come up out of the river.

As soon as this command was obeyed, when the priests' feet touched dry ground, immediately the waters of the Jordan returned to their place as they had been before, still overflowing the banks as before.

So the water stood off immediately when the priests' feet touched it and then came back immediately when their feet left it. All this happened by God's command, proving clearly to the people that it was a miracle by God's power.

4:19-24 – The stones taken from the river were set up in Gilgal as a memorial so future generations would know that Israel crossed the Jordan on dry ground.

The people completed crossing the Jordan on the tenth day of the first month of the year. They camped in an area that was known as Gilgal (see **map**). This was near Jericho, but obviously quite close to the river. See 5:9.

There Joshua took the stones the twelve men had carried up out of the river, and he set them up as a memorial as God had commanded. Again the people were told the purpose of the stones. When future generations saw the stones and asked about them, the people were to tell them these were put there as a memorial of the time the people crossed the Jordan on dry ground.

The people would thereby be reminded that God had dried up the Jordan River, just as He had enabled the people to cross the Red Sea on dry ground. The purpose of the memorial was to remind them of the miracle. And the purpose of the miracle was to prove to them the power of God, so they would respect and fear Him forever.

This demonstrates two purposes of miracles. They served to convince people to believe that the God of the Bible exists and is the true God. They also served to convince people to recognize men through whom God worked as being really from God – Joshua in this case – because they were the ones through whom God's power was demonstrated. Of course, still a third purpose (not referred to here) is to convince us to believe that the Bible is the word of God, since this is the book which records these miracles and was written by these inspired men.

Joshua 5

Circumcision of Males –
Joshua 5:1-12

5:1 – The hearts of the people of the land melted when they heard how Israel had crossed the Jordan.

When Israel had approached Canaan the first time forty years earlier, they had refused to enter because they feared the people of the land. But this time we are told that the people of the land feared Israel.

Rahab had told the spies that the people feared, because they had heard about the crossing of the Red Sea and the defeat of the people east of the Jordan (compare 2:10,11). Now, in addition, the kings and the people west of Jordan heard how God had enabled the people to miraculously cross the Jordan. This led them to fear even further. The account says their hearts melted and they had no spirit in them – i.e., no courage to resist.

This demonstrates a further purpose for miracles. They produce faith in God among those, like Israel and Rahab, who have hearts honest and willing to trust in God. But even those who resist God's will are affected. Their conviction that they are right is weakened. They may not be converted to follow the Lord and may not cease resisting truth, but they are at least weakened in their stand for error.

5:2-7 – God commanded Joshua to circumcise the men who had not been circumcised during the wilderness wandering.

God told Joshua to make flint knives and use them to circumcise all the males among Israel. Joshua did so at a place then called the hill of foreskins.

Study Notes on Joshua and Ruth

The reason this was needed is that the younger generation had not been circumcised. Those who had left Egypt had been circumcised. But that generation had died on the way due to their disobedience in not entering Canaan at their first opportunity. They had refused to enter the land and so were consumed during the years of wandering.

The younger generation – the children who were born as Israel traveled in the wilderness after they left Egypt – had not been circumcised. They still needed this to be done, so it was done at this time.

Circumcision was the sign of being a descendant of Abraham and an heir of the promise to Abraham. See Genesis 17; Exodus 4:25; 12:43-48; Leviticus 12:3. It was clearly required by God both before and after the giving of the law at Mt. Sinai.

So one wonders why it had not previously been done to the younger generation. Verse 7 says they did not do it while traveling. Surely it would have been inconvenient. But it was done to males eight days old, so it seems it could have been done at that age without serious problem.

It may be that God simply did not insist on the practice in these difficult circumstances. However, the older generation clearly had rebelled against God and had been rejected by Him. Perhaps in their rebellion they simply did not keep other basic commands, including circumcision. Moses had been among them, and one would think that he would teach them the truth. Perhaps, however, God had not bothered to lead Moses to insist on this, since God had rejected that generation anyway.

5:8,9 – The people rested after the circumcision, and God said He had rolled away the reproach of Egypt.

Circumcision is a painful procedure at any age, but baby boys can heal rather quickly. And they cannot do anything for themselves in the meanwhile anyway, so no great loss is caused if the procedure is done at that age. However, when grown men are circumcised, they are incapacitated for work for several days, and they surely are not fit for war. So God had these men stay in camp for several days till they were healed.

One wonders why God waited till this time to have this done. They were near their enemies and were basically defenseless for several days (though the enemies would not likely know this). Had this been done east of Jordan it would have been safer. There their enemies were already defeated, and any enemies from west of Jordan would have had to cross the river to attack. God's reasons for waiting are not stated. Perhaps it was a test of faith to see if Israel would obey even when facing danger.

Then God said that He had rolled away from them the reproach of Egypt, so the place was named Gilgal (meaning "rolling"). Other passages refer to Gilgal. It is not clear whether they are the same or different locations. 4:19,20 had referred to it by this name, but apparently that account was written after the name had been given here at this event recorded in chapter 5.

What was the reproach of Egypt? I am not sure. Being uncircumcised was surely a reproach, especially for descendants of Abraham (compare Gen. 34:14). And this reproach was removed when they were circumcised. They were about to eat the Passover, and the males had to be circumcised in order to eat it (Ex. 12:43-48).

But what had this to do with Egypt? Perhaps the point was that this generation was obedient to God unlike the previous generation had been. Perhaps God had viewed the previous generation with reproach as He had viewed the Egyptians. Or perhaps their failure to enter the land had brought the reproach of the people of Egypt on them (compare Zeph. 2:8). God had delivered them from slavery in Egypt, but until now He had not fulfilled the promise to bring them into the land of Canaan. When they finally entered the land, the people had finally been delivered from the reproach of being slaves in Egypt.

In any case, this generation had kept God's word, so He had given them a renewal of the covenant of circumcision. This indicated they were truly His people, thereby removing the reproach that had been on their parents' generation.

5:10-12 – Israel observed the Passover. The manna ceased when they ate the produce of the land.

At Gilgal Israel also kept the Passover on the 14th day of the first month of the year. This is what God had commanded as recorded in Exodus 12:6. God had instituted the Passover as a memorial to the time He had slain the firstborn of the Egyptian sons but had "passed over" the firstborn of the Israelites, sparing them because they had put blood on their doors.

Israel was to keep this memorial every year. They had kept it sometimes (Num. 9:5), but it is not clear if they had kept it regularly as God commanded. Perhaps they had neglected this in their rebellion, even as they had neglected circumcision. Now they were returning to God's service, so they kept circumcision then the Passover. They had to be circumcised first in order to take the Passover properly (see above).

Study Notes on Joshua and Ruth

It is interesting that renewing their spiritual service to God took precedence even over conquering the inhabitants of the land. Those who want the blessings of God in their lives, must put priority on their relationship to God. Only when we seek first the will of God and our relationship with Him do we have the promise of His blessings on our lives.

The food of the land and the end of the manna

Following the Passover was to be a feast of seven days in which bread had to be unleavened. After this celebration of the Passover, Israel ate bread unleavened along with parched grain and other foods. But what was special about this was that for the first time they had eaten the fruit of the land of Canaan. Until this they had been outside the land. Now they had entered and intended to obey God's command to take the land. They enjoyed eating the fruit of the land as God had promised them.

Since they had then come into the land, the manna ceased. The manna had provided their need for food throughout the forty years of wandering in the wilderness (compare Exodus 16, especially v35). But now that they were in the promised land, they were able to eat the fruit of this land and did not need the manna. So it ceased.

This demonstrates an important Biblical principle about miracles: God never continues miracles after their purpose has been completed. Many people claim that God must do miracles today because He has done them in the past. But the record of all Biblical miracles demonstrates that they continued only as long as they serve a necessary purpose according to the plan of God. Then they ceased. Consider, for example the miracles of creation, the flood, the crossing of the Red Sea, the resurrection of Jesus from the dead, etc. But the purpose of *all* miracles was completed when the Scriptures were completed, so they ceased (1 Corinthians 13:8-11).

For further information about the duration of miracles, see our articles on miracles and direct revelation today at our Bible Instruction web site at **www.gospelway.com/instruct/**.

Archaeology and the Israelite invasion of Canaan

For many years, liberal scholars have attempted to deny that Israel ever conquered Canaan in the time of Joshua, because they found little confirmation outside the Scriptures. Of course, the Scriptures are enough for those who believe in the inspiration of the word of God on the basis of eyewitness testimony of miracles, fulfilled prophecy, and the resurrection of Jesus. However, archaeology does have value in giving secondary confirmation of many Biblical accounts.

Joseph Free offers the following evidence to confirm the conquest of Canaan in Joshua's day.

> The Amarna Tablets comprise a group of letters written by the kings of various Palestinian and Syrian cities to the two kings of Egypt who lived about 1400 B.C. ... Several of the Amarna Tablets tell of the invasion of a group called the Habiri. Many scholars believe that the Habiri are to be identified with the Hebrews under Joshua ... , And it is quite likely that the Amarna Tablets give a reflection of the conquest from the standpoint of the native dwellers of Canaan.

Free also lists several cities that the book of Joshua says the Israelites captured and which have also been excavated. This includes Jericho, Lachish, Debir, and Hazor. He states that evidence has been found for each of these cities indicating they were destroyed around the time of Joshua. On the other hand, the account indicates several other cities were not captured in the time of Joshua, and excavation of these cities confirms that they were not destroyed at this time. (See also Millard, p92.)

Study Notes on Joshua and Ruth

Part 2: Israel Conquers Canaan (Joshua 5:13- chapter 12)

Conquest of Jericho – Joshua 5:13-chapter6

5:13-15 - The Commander of the Army of the Lord

5:13-15 – The Commander of the Lord's army appeared to Joshua and said to take off his sandals because he stood on holy ground.

Joshua stood by Jericho, apparently across from it looking at the place where they must fight their first battle. Jericho was a major fortified city standing between them and taking the land.

As he so stood, he saw what appeared to be a man standing opposite him having His sword drawn in His hand. Joshua approached him and asked if he was for the Israelite army or for their enemies. Perhaps he was asking which army the man was a member of, since the man answered "No" – i.e., he was not actually a member of either army. Instead, He explained that He was the Commander of the army of the Lord who had come. Obviously He was on Joshua's side, but was a member of the Lord's army, not either of the human armies.

Joshua fell on his face and worshipped and asked what the Lord wanted to say to him. He viewed himself as a servant and correctly concluded that this One had appeared with a message for him. Joshua was about to enter into the first battle that he had actually directed as the highest leader of the people (though he had led many times subject to Moses). God had been guiding and instructing Joshua in many ways since he took command of the Israelites. So he was looking for God's further guidance, especially regarding taking Jericho.

The Commander of the Lord's army told him to take off his sandals, since he was standing on holy ground. Joshua obeyed. This, of course, is the same thing God had told Moses when He had appeared to him in the burning bush to call him to lead Israel from Egypt (Exodus 3:5). This event, so clearly similar to what happened with Moses, was another evidence that God was really using Joshua to lead the people. God wanted both Joshua and the people to know that Joshua was the appointed leader whom all should follow.

Two facts would indicate that this was not just a man but was actually God appearing in the form of a man: (1) the fact Joshua actually worshipped Him, and (2) the instruction to take off his sandals as Moses had been instructed when in the presence of God at the burning bush. It would seem that God here appeared in the form of a man, just as He had appeared in the bush to Moses. For other examples consider Gen. 18:1-33; 32:24-30; Ex. 3:2ff (see also Num. 22:31-35; Gen. 16:7-13; 21:17; 22:11-18; 24:7,40; 31:11; 48:15,16; Judges 6:11-24; 13:3-23; etc.

But what was the purpose of this visit of the Commander of the Lord's army? One purpose would surely be to confirm that Joshua was the leader God had chosen to lead Israel into battle, even as God's appearance to Moses confirmed that Moses was to lead God's people. This served the purpose of all miracles. Another purpose would be to give encouragement and strength to Joshua as he faced his first battle as leader of God's people. He would need assurance that God would be with Him (see on 1:5-9).

But another purpose of the meeting appears to me to be to give Joshua instructions about how to approach the upcoming battle. Joshua asked the Commander what He had to say to Joshua. He needed instruction and was evidently expecting to receive them. Chapter 5, however, records no such instructions. If we ignore the chapter division that men inserted, however, chapter 6 begins almost immediately giving the instructions of God for taking Jericho. It appears to me that the message from God in 6:2-5 is the message given by this Commander to Joshua. He appeared in 5:13-15, but what He told Joshua is actually recorded in chapter 6.

Study Notes on Joshua and Ruth

Joshua 6

Joshua 6 - Fall of Jericho

6:1-5 — God said the wall of Jericho would fall if the men would march around it once a day for six days then seven times on the seventh day, blow horns, and shout.

Jericho feared the Israelites so that they sought security behind their walls. They were shut in so that no one could go in or out of the city. This was typical of walled cities that were besieged, but Jericho was especially sure to do so because of their fear of Israel.

God then gave Joshua instructions for how they would defeat the city despite the wall. These were most likely the instructions given by the Commander of the Lord's host in 5:13-15.

God began by saying that He had given Jericho with its king and powerful defenders all into Joshua's hand. Note that this was a gift from God (compare v16). We will see how it was given as the story proceeds. But God clearly states that it was a gift. The people did not, by their deeds or actions, deserve or merit receiving the gift. They did not labor so hard as to earn the defeat of the city.

The Israelite men of war were commanded to march around Jericho once each day for six days. This, of course, would be a foolish way to capture a city, except for the fact that God said to do it. Hebrews 11:30 says the walls fell down by faith. The people were required to have enough trust in God to destroy the walls that they were willing to seek the victory according to His will. But this still required obedience.

Furthermore, seven priests were to carry seven trumpets made from rams' horns before the ark (the ark was to be carried among the soldiers as they marched about the city). As they had marched one time each day for six days, on the seventh day they were to march seven times and the priests were to blow the trumpets and all the people were to shout. Then God promised the wall would fall down flat, and all the people could march directly into the city.

This did require faith. But it also constituted a miraculous sign. Such a means of causing a wall to fall is clearly impossible by natural law. It could happen only by the supernatural power of God. As such, it would serve the purpose of all miracles. It would confirm the existence and power of God as the true God, and it would confirm to Israel and to the people of the land that Joshua was truly a leader sent from God. The people should then respect him and follow his commands.

As a matter of interest, note that in so marching, Israel must have done "work" on the Sabbath day. They marched once each day for six days then seven times on the seventh day. No matter what day of the week they began, they must have marched on the Sabbath. Of course, this was done by God's express command, so it was not a sin. But we can learn that God never intended the Sabbath to forbid all work of all kinds. During His lifetime, Jesus often had conflict with the Jewish leaders over this subject. They frequently criticized Him and His disciples for violating their traditions about the Sabbath day. However, Jesus repeatedly showed them that not all that could technically be considered as work was forbidden on the Sabbath.

6:6-10 – The men were to march without speaking, but the priests were blow trumpets till the time came to shout.

Joshua then gave the commands of God to the people to follow in marching. These instructions were as described in verses 3-5, but some additional information is given.

For one thing, we are told that, not only did the seven priests with the trumpets precede the ark, but so did many of the soldiers. However, there was also a rear guard marching after the ark.

Further, the priests continued blowing the trumpets as they marched around the city (verses 9,13). But the people were not to shout or make any noise with their voices until the command was given to shout. This would be on the seventh day after the seventh circuit of the city. They would shout at the time when Joshua commanded them to shout.

Note how specific and clear the instructions were. Faith was required, but so was obedience. Suppose Israel had disobeyed the rules. Would they have received the benefit? So, the faith that God blessed was obedient faith, and without the obedience they would never have taken the city.

Study Notes on Joshua and Ruth

The fall of Jericho illustrates our salvation by faith.

Note that the walls of Jericho fell by "faith," but Israel had to act to receive the blessing (Hebrews 11:30). Yet God said He **gave** Jericho to Israel (Josh 6:2). Likewise, the gospel of Christ teaches that salvation is a gift, so some say that there is nothing to do to receive it. So they conclude that baptism is not necessary to salvation.

But God's gifts are often conditional. We must act, but our actions are inadequate to **earn or merit** the result. The action required does not earn the blessing God offers, but it constitutes a test of faith to see whether or not we will obey even when God's command makes little human sense.

Israel received Jericho as a gift from God "by faith," but they still had to obey to receive it. So Ephesians 2:8,9 says salvation is a gift from God "by faith." This does not prove there is nothing to do. It just proves that our actions do not **earn** the gift, so we cannot boast.

Salvation by grace through faith does not exclude baptism. It requires it. See Mark 16:15,16; Acts 2:38; 22:16; Romans 6:3,4; Galatians 3:27; 1 Peter 3:21.

For further information, see our articles on the importance of baptism and salvation by faith only or by obedient faith at our Bible Instruction web site at **www.gospelway.com/instruct/**.

6:11-14 – Israel marched around the city as God had commanded.

So Joshua had the people with the ark encircle the city as God commanded. On the first day, they marched with the ark once around the city. Then they returned to camp.

Then on the next day they got up early in the morning and took the ark and circled the city again. The priests blew the horns as they marched, as God had commanded. They did the same thing each day for six days.

6:15-19 – Israel marched seven times on the seventh day, the priests blew the trumpets, and the people shouted. God said the people should keep no spoils.

On the seventh day, Joshua and the people arose early about dawn and marched around the city seven times, as God had commanded. On that day, when the priests blew the trumpets, Joshua for the first time commanded the people to shout, since God had given the city to them (compare v2).

Instructions regarding the plunder

Joshua told the people not to keep any of the spoils of the city for themselves. Everything was doomed either to be destroyed or else to be given to the service of God. The people were all to be slain except for Rahab's family, because she had believed in God and had helped the spies (chapter 2). All the silver, gold, and vessels of bronze or iron were to be given to the Lord by placing them into the treasury of the Lord. If the people kept anything for themselves, they would bring a curse upon the camp.

It is likely that these instructions had been given to Israel earlier and were just recorded here (although Joshua could have been repeating them at this time).

At cities captured later, the people were allowed to keep spoils for themselves. Why was Jericho an exception? Probably this was because it was the first city captured, so God's law of the firstfruits prevailed. The firstborn son in each family and the firstfruits of each crop belonged to God (Ex. 23:19; 34:26). Most likely God made a similar rule regarding Jericho to remind the people this was so.

Some have questioned the justice of God in destroying all the people of the city. But this is what God had commanded from the beginning. See our introductory notes to the book. God commanded Israel, not just to take the lands of these people, but to utterly destroy them and their idols. Otherwise, the Israelites would be influenced by these people to commit idolatry with their gods (Deut. 7:1-6; 9:1-5; 20:10-18).

These nations had been wicked for many years, but earlier they had not been wicked enough for God to demand their complete destruction (Gen. 15:16). So He waited in justice. But now their iniquity was "full." God had determined that they had become so corrupt that the only way to remove their evil influence was to slay them all. We will later see that Israel only partially fulfilled this command, resulting in exactly the problems God predicted.

6:20-23 – When the wall fell, the people destroyed everyone, keeping no spoils. Only Rahab's family was spared.

As God had commanded, after the people had circled the city for the seventh time, the priests sounded the trumpets and the people shouted. The walls fell down flat, then each man went straight before him to take the city. They then utterly destroyed every living thing in the city, people and animals, as God had commanded.

However, Rahab and her family were spared as the spies had agreed with her. Joshua had told the spies to go to her house and bring out everyone who was with her there (see on chapter 2). It sounds as though somehow this was done before the wall fell. Her house was on the wall, so it does not seem that it could have survived the fall of the wall. In any case, by whatever means, the Israelites spared her and everyone with her in the house.

6:24-27 – The city was burned and valuable spoils put into the treasury of the tabernacle. Joshua pronounced a curse on whoever rebuilt the city.

The city itself was then burned with fire. But the silver, gold, and vessels of bronze and iron were put into the treasury for caring for the house of God (the tabernacle). As God had commanded, the people were to take none of the spoils (but note on chapter 7).

Rahab and family were spared, as the messengers had promised. When the book of Joshua was written, Rahab continued even then to live in Israel.

Curse on any who would rebuild the city

Joshua then pronounced a curse on any man who would rebuild the city of Jericho. Specifically, his firstborn would die when the foundation of the city was laid, and his youngest would die when the gates were set up.

This curse was exactly fulfilled many years later, as recorded in 1 Kings 16:34. A man named Hiel of Bethel rebuilt Jericho. His firstborn Abiram died when the foundation was laid, and his youngest son Segub died when the gates were set up.

Joshua was highly respected in his day among the people, because God was with him. This event also proves that he was a prophet, for his prediction came true. His miracles and fulfilled prophecies proved that God spoke through him, which is the purpose of these miraculous gifts.

Archaeology, Jericho, and Ai

The confirmation of the fall of Jericho and Ai by archaeologists has been controversial. According to Joseph Free, Garstang excavated Jericho in the 1930s. He claimed that his discoveries confirmed the Bible account of the fall of Jericho. However, a later well-known archaeologist disputed his results. Today, many scholars deny the accuracy of the Bible record of the fall of Jericho and Ai.

Dr. Bryant Wood of the Associates for Biblical Research (ABR) has done extensive studies regarding Jericho and Ai. He presents convincing evidence that Garstang's conclusions regarding Jericho were correct, and the later excavations were mistaken because they ignored his primary evidence. Likewise, Wood claims that recent archaeologists have reached mistaken conclusions about Ai because they incorrectly identified its location. His research strongly supports the accuracy of the Biblical account. Since these are ongoing studies, rather than summarize them here, I urge interested readers to study the evidence presented on the website of ABR at www.biblearchaeology.org.

Joshua 7

Sin of Achan & Defeat of Ai - Joshua 7&8

Joshua 7 - Sin of Achan

Israel had defeated Jericho by God's command and was ready to move on to the next city, which was Ai. Fresh from an overwhelming victory, they were ready for another easy victory. However, problems were waiting that they did not expect.

7:1 – Achan took for himself some of the spoils from Jericho that should have been destroyed or given to the tabernacle treasury.

The account begins by telling about Achan's sin. The sin is described later in much more detail. We are told about it before the account of the attack on Ai, so we understand what happened. However, Israel at this point knew nothing about why the problem would occur.

Achan of the tribe of Judah had sinned in taking some of the spoils of Jericho. This had been expressly forbidden. All was to be destroyed or given to the tabernacle treasury. Achan's sin brought trouble to the whole nation.

One wonders why the passage says "the children of Israel" sinned and God was angry with them (compare v11). Only one man sinned and the others knew nothing about it. Does this mean He held them all guilty, or is it just an expression for the fact that sin was found in their midst and they were all about to suffer for it? (See further notes below.)

7:2-5 – 3000 men sent to capture Ai were soundly defeated, and the people became greatly discouraged.

The next town to be taken in Israel's path was Ai, apparently a relatively small city. We are told that it was beside Beth Aven, east of Bethel. But it was west and a little north from Jericho (see **map**).

As he had done at Jericho, Joshua sent spies to determine what means should be taken to capture Ai. The spies returned with a confident report that the city was so small that only two or three thousand men would be needed, so there was no need to trouble the whole army.

So three thousand went up against Ai, but the people of Ai defeated them. Israel fled and 36 men were struck down. They fled as far as Shebarim (location unknown). The result was great discouragement among the Israelites.

One wonders whether Joshua and Israel made mistakes here, perhaps even sinning. First, they seem almost overconfident. Fresh from such a great and easy victory over a strongly fortified city at Jericho, perhaps they thought Ai would be no problem at all.

Furthermore, Joshua had carefully sought God's guidance each step of the way till now. But here there is no mention of any prayer or consultation with God about His will. Surely had they consulted Him first, as they had been doing, He would have guided them. See on 9:14. Surely this guidance would have included a warning about Achan's sin, and this would in turn have avoided the whole defeat. One wonders whether or not this is the sense in which verse 1 means Israel had sinned. Or perhaps this was just poor judgment on their part.

In any case, we learn here that times of prosperity can be a source of trouble to God's people as surely as can times of hardship. When we suffer, we tend to be discouraged and lose faith. When all goes well, we tend to be self-confident and fail to appreciate our need to trust God. Blessings and troubles can both be a cause of downfall, if we do not use them properly.

7:6-9 – Joshua asked God why they entered the land if they were going to be defeated by their enemies.

Joshua grieved deeply over the defeat. He tore his clothes and put dust on his head as customary signs of grief. He fell before the ark until evening, along with the elders of Israel.

Then he raised his complaint to God why this great loss had occurred. He asked whether God had brought Israel into the land only to have them destroyed at the hands of their enemies. He thought they would have been better off had they simply stayed on the east side of Jordan.

Study Notes on Joshua and Ruth

Then he wondered what would happen when the people of the land heard that Israel had fled in battle and from such an apparently weak enemy. He thought the enemies might surround Israel, now that they were in the land, and destroy them. This would not only be tragic for the people, but it would also bring reproach on God's name. As Henry points out, when things go against them, even good men are apt to fear the worst.

If Joshua had not consulted God before the attack, he surely did here! Troubles can humble us to see our need for God, whereas we might not see that need when all goes well.

Yet Joshua seems almost to be complaining and murmuring against God, much like the nation had done in the wilderness whenever things did not go well. His faith seems to be shaken and perhaps worse. The account does not directly say he sinned here, but God is about to respond to him forcefully in the following verses. In any case, had Joshua gone to God for guidance before the attack, surely the defeat at least could have been avoided.

7:10-12 – God explained that Israel could not stand before their enemies because they had taken for themselves some of the devoted spoils of Jericho.

God's response commanded Joshua to get up and asked why he was lying on his face. The response seems to imply that Joshua should have known better than to think God had in any way failed. We need to learn this lesson too. When things do not go well, it is not God's fault. Don't blame Him. Usually people are to blame to some extent, or perhaps it is Satan. But God is not to blame.

In this case God explained that Israel had sinned, as described in verse 1. They had transgressed the covenant by taking some of the devoted spoils of Jericho and keeping it for themselves, which God had forbidden in 6:17-19. God calls this stealing and deception. And it was stealing from God at that! The devoted things were supposed to go to the worship and service of God. Anyone who kept them for himself, was attempting to steal what belongs to God.

God said this was the reason Israel was defeated by their enemies. The sin had doomed them to destruction. And what was more, they would continue to be defeated unless they dealt with the sin and removed the devoted property. God would not be with them as long as they harbored sinners among themselves.

Lessons about sin

Clearly we learn here the dangers of sin and disobedience to God's covenant. God cannot bless those who sin against Him. He may continue to send the common blessings that He sends on all mankind, but He extends no special protection and blessing that He offers to His people.

Furthermore, we must learn that sins we commit create problems for other people too. Israel in general had not stolen the devoted things. Just one man did that. People today often think, "It's my life. It's no one else's business what I do. If what I do brings consequences, that's my problem. It's my own personal business." But sooner or later sin creates problems for other people too. It may be a bad influence leading other people also to justify their sins. It may cause suffering and hardship on our loved ones. But if nothing else, it hinders God's ability to bless those with whom we associate.

Furthermore, we see here that, when God's people learn about sin among the members of the group, they are responsible to deal with it. They must not simply ignore it, or God will not bless them. God cannot fellowship those in sin, including those who justify sin in others. God said He would not dwell among the nation until they dealt with the problem. We must take care to avoid sin in the camp. See also 2 John 9-11; Ephesians 5:11; Proverbs 17:15; 2 Corinthians 6:17-7:1; 1 Timothy 5:22; Psalms 1:1,2; 1 Corinthians 15:33; Romans 1:32; Acts 7:58; 8:1; 22:20.

Other lessons to be learned include the fact that we cannot hide from God. He knows our sins and will surely punish if we do not repent (see notes below for more on these points.)

7:13-15 – God said to determine who was guilty, then he and all that belonged to him should be burned.

If Israel had not known before what the problem was and what to do about it, they surely learned here! God told Joshua to inform the people and warn them about the problem. They were to sanctify themselves in preparation for the next day – make themselves holy (see on 3:5). He was to tell them, as God had told him, that the problem was sin in the camp. There was devoted property among them, and they could not prosper in their battles until they removed those spoils.

God then told Joshua how to handle the matter the next day. He was to have the people come before them so God could indicate what tribe, then what family, household, and finally what man was guilty. This one was to be taken, along with the devoted spoils, and be burned along with all his family, because of his sin against God and the terrible influence he had.

Lessons about dealing with sin

One wonders how Achan spent that night! Surely he knew he was guilty. Presumably he did not believe the people could find out

Study Notes on Joshua and Ruth

and punish him. But he surely knew that he was guilty, even if no one else knew.

God had commanded the people to sanctify themselves. Surely Achan knew he needed to make himself holy, and God's command showed that required eliminating the devoted things. If he had come at that point confessing his deed, one wonders if the punishment would have been less severe. Perhaps God delayed till the next day to give him time to make correction. In any case, Achan made no correction, so his punishment was clearly justified when it did come. If we want mercy, we need to confess our errors and make correction while we have the opportunity.

Furthermore, this demonstrates the need for God's people to take disciplinary action against sin among the group. It is not enough for others just to refuse to commit the same sin, nor is it enough to speak against it. If speaking does not lead to repentance, the group must take action against sin.

The New Testament likewise requires that God's church must discipline those who sin and do not repent. If we fail, then we become the sinners. See 1 Corinthians 5; 2 Thessalonians 3:6,14,15; Matthew 18:15-17; Titus 3:10,11; Romans 16:17,18; 1 Timothy 1:3-11,19,20; 2 Corinthians 2:6-11; 2 John 9-11; Hebrews 12:15; 1 Corinthians 15:33.

7:16-19 – Investigation discovered Achan to be guilty, so Joshua called upon him to confess.

On the next day, Joshua did as God had commanded. He brought each tribe forth and Judah was taken. Then the family and household were indicated. Finally, Achan was demonstrated to be the guilty man.

Joshua then commanded Achan to make confession, telling what he had done without hiding it. In this way he would honor and glorify God. It always glorifies God when we admit He is right and just, even if we must do so by admitting we are wrong. This would demonstrate that God had not failed the people (as Joshua, and no doubt other people, thought He had). Rather, there was justifiable reason for what God had done.

Joshua's response to Achan was almost surprisingly mild. This man had committed a grievous sin against God and against the nation. Joshua could easily have forcefully and powerfully rebuked him. Yet Joshua referred to him as his son and appears to have spoken almost with compassion. At this point, there was no doubt about Achan's guilt or about the punishment that God had required he must receive. His fate was sealed. And while it is proper for us to seek for justice to be done when people are guilty of sin and refuse to repent, we ought also to have a sense of grief wishing that instead they had avoided the sin in the first place or at least repented of it so they could be forgiven.

We are not here told exactly what method was used by God to indicate which tribe, family, etc., was chosen. Similar events occurred elsewhere, as in 1 Samuel 14:38-42 (compare 10:19-22). In 1 Samuel 14 we are told that the method used was casting lots (compare Acts 1:24-26). Perhaps in other cases other methods were used. In any case, the point is that this was a revelation from God.

Achan probably thought, as many people think today, that he could hide from God. They think people cannot find out what they did, so no one can know. But God knows all things. No sin can escape Him, so we should be sure that our sin will be found out and punished – Num. 23:23. See Proverbs 3:19; Psalm 139:1-4,6-12; 147:4,5; John 16:30; Matthew 10:29-31; 6:8,32; 1 Kings 8:39; Romans 11:33,34; Isaiah 55:8,9.

7:20-23 – Achan had taken silver, gold, and a garment and had hidden them in his tent. A search found the forbidden items.

Seeing that he was caught, Achan finally confessed openly his sin. Specifically, he identified the devoted things he had stolen to be a Babylonian garment, 200 shekels of silver (perhaps five pounds) and 50 shekels of gold. He said he coveted and took them and hid them in the dirt in the midst of his tent.

Joshua sent messengers to Achan's tent. There they found the items, exactly as Achan had admitted. They brought them and laid them in the presence of Joshua, the Lord, and all Israel.

Covetousness is greed: an overly strong desire that leads us to be willing to obtain things in an unauthorized or improper way. In this case, it was improper to take any of the spoils from Jericho, but Achan's covetousness led him to keep them. See other verses about greed and over-emphasis on material things: Matthew 6:19-33; 16:24-27; Romans 8:5-8; 12:1,2; 2 Corinthians 8:5; 10:3,4; John 6:27,63; Luke 12:15-21; 1 Timothy 6:6-10; Colossians 3:1,2.

Greed is especially strange in that it may lead us to desire and take that which we cannot really even use. What good did that Babylonian garment do Achan while buried in the dirt under his tent? Could he wear it without people asking where he got it? Could he sell it or give it as a gift? How could he even use the silver or gold without arousing questions? Perhaps he thought he could take these things with him and later use them in some way. But the guilt and secrecy in the meanwhile were surely not worth it. And how much

Study Notes on Joshua and Ruth

better everyone would have been had he obeyed God's command to begin with!

Notice that the sin began with the eyes, then moved to the heart, and finally showed itself in conduct. Achan said that he saw these items and then he coveted them. His eyes were the avenue by which the temptation entered his heart. See 1 John 2:15-17 and consider the temptation of Eve. Then his heart desired them, and finally he gave in. Sin tempts us by appealing to our desires, but it becomes sin when we give in and allow it to lead us to do, say, or think that which violates God's law. See James 1:14,15.

Then observe the clear statement of his sin that Achan made when he did confess. He identified exactly what his guilt was. Far too often people know they are guilty and what it was that they did wrong. Other people may know as well. And yet those who are guilty often want to make some minimal confession that as much as possible hides their true guilt. They may say, "If I have said or done anything that may have hurt someone's feelings..." Such a confession does not actually admit guilt and surely does not acknowledge what the sin was. Those who are truly penitent need to benefit from the example of Achan's confession.

7:24-26 – Israel stoned Achan and burned all his family and possessions, including the forbidden spoils.

Joshua then commanded Israel to take those devoted things, Achan himself, and all his family and his possessions to a valley called the valley of Achor (location unknown). There Israel stoned him, as God had commanded, then they burned them with fire and raised a great heap of stones over them. That heap still existed when the book was written. This satisfied God's justice and His anger was taken away.

Joshua said Achan had troubled Israel, so the Lord would trouble Him. "Achan" means "trouble," so he was rightly named. "Achor" also means "troubling." Presumably this name was given to the valley after this event. So the place of punishment became a symbol and a memorial to the trouble caused by sin.

Again the event shows God's determination that sin must be removed from among His people. We are responsible to deal with it, even though we did not commit it.

One wonders why Achan's sons and daughters were also slain. God had commanded that the sons were not to be put to death for the sin of the father – Deut. 24:16; 2 Kings 14:6; (Ezek. 18:20). On the other hand, in Numbers 16:25-35 the families of Dathan and Abiram died with them for their sin, and this is what God had commanded to be done in Achan's case (7:15). I can only conclude that Achan's family was aware of his sin and would not stand against him or in some other way God knew they too were worthy of punishment.

Joshua 8

8:1-29 - Defeat of Ai

8:1,2 — God promised to give Ai to Israel. They should take all the people of war and lay an ambush, then they could take the spoil for themselves.

Since Israel had eliminated sin from its midst, God was ready to bless the nation again. He promised Joshua that there was no longer any reason for fear. The previous defeat at Ai may have given Joshua and the people great reason to be fearful and hesitant. But God here affirmed that, since the reason for the first defeat had been eliminated, He would give Ai and everything pertaining to it into Joshua's hand.

This time, however, they were not to send just two or three thousand men. They were to take the whole army against the city. God then promised that they would defeat Ai and its king as surely as they had defeated Jericho and its king.

He further added that this time the spoils would belong to the people. At Jericho the spoils had belonged to God, probably because it was the firstfruits of the land captured by Israel as earlier explained. It was this command that Achan had violated that led to defeat at Ai the first time. Whatever the reason for the change, God clearly said that the spoils of this city belonged to the people.

Note that Achan sought to take spoils that God had forbidden, so he died. Had he been willing to wait until Israel attacked the next city, he would have shared in the spoils with those who were obedient.

God gave some further instruction, however, about how the battle should be conducted. He said they were to lay an ambush behind the city. We will see how this worked as the story proceeds.

Note that, unlike the first attack on Ai, this time we are expressly told that Joshua was consulting God and God was instructing him regarding the conduct of the battle. Had Joshua so consulted God before the first attack on Ai, the previous defeat could have been avoided.

8:3-8 – Joshua set an ambush behind the city. The main army would flee as before, and when the people of Ai pursued them, the ambush should capture the city.

Further details are given here for the plan of the ambush. Joshua sent soldiers away by night to an area behind the city. They were to stay hidden but close to the city, ready to attack at Joshua's command.

Joshua would take other men and would attack the city like it had been attacked at the previous defeat. When the men of Ai came out to fight, Joshua and his men would then flee again as they had done the first time. This would draw the men of Ai away from the protection of their city. But this time as Israel fled, the men of ambush would enter the city and capture it and set it on fire.

This is what God commanded, so Joshua so commanded the people. He assured them this time they would be successful, because they had God's blessings and assurance of success.

8:9-12 – Joshua sent the ambush into position by night, then he and the main army approached the city from a different direction.

So Joshua sent them away, presumably referring to the 30,000 soldiers of verse 3. They placed an ambush on the west side of Ai, between Ai and Bethel. Presumably they went by night so the people of Ai would not know they had moved into ambush.

Joshua, however, stayed in the camp among the people. Then early the next morning, he and all the rest of the people went to the north of Ai and made camp there, with a valley between them and Ai.

We are then told about a group of 5000 men who were set in ambush between Bethel and Ai on the west side of Ai. This is somewhat confusing. This is where the 30,000 of verses 3-9 were sent. Why send these 5000 there?

I can think of only four possibilities. (1) Joshua decided the 30,000 were not enough, so he later sent still more. (2) He wanted two groups in the same area, perhaps to move in from slightly different directions, at different times, or to accomplish different goals. (3) The 30,000 were the whole group that would attack the city, including the 5000. The whole 30,000 had the plan explained to them, then 5000 were chosen to set the ambush. This explanation, however, does not seem to fit the language. Besides, the whole army was to attack Ai (verses 1,3), and that would include far more than 30,000 men (in Numbers 26:51 the men of war numbered over 600,000). (4) We will learn later that the men of Bethel joined the men of Ai in this battle. Perhaps the 5000 were to attack Bethel as the 30,000 attacked Ai.

Or perhaps there is some other alternative I do not understand.

8:13-17 – When the army of Ai came out to fight, Israel fled and all the men of Ai were drawn away from the city.

After all the soldiers were in position, those on the west and those on the north, Joshua moved with his men into the valley at night. When the king of Ai saw this, he aroused his soldiers early the following morning for a battle in the plain. But he was still unaware of the ambush.

As planned, Joshua's men acted as though they were beaten, so they fled toward the wilderness. The people of Ai "took the bait" and followed them, clearly thinking they could defeat Israel like they had the first time. In fact, all the men of the city and of Bethel joined in the pursuit of Israel, so no one was left in the city at all. They left the city "open" – either undefended or perhaps even with the gates open.

Note that the men of Bethel joined in the pursuit. Perhaps they had been already in Ai with a treaty or agreement of some kind to join in the defense of Ai. They probably knew they were next, if Ai fell. So they had already entered Ai to join together in the fight.

8:18-23 – At the signal of Joshua, the ambush took the city and set it on fire. Then Israel turned against the men of Ai, surrounded, and defeated them.

God then commanded Joshua to stretch out his spear toward Ai. He promised He would then give the city to Joshua and Israel. So Joshua stretched out his spear as God had commanded.

Note the similarity between this and other events. Moses stretched forth his rod to begin various plagues on Egypt (Ex. 8:6,16). Later Moses held out the staff so the Red Sea would open to Israel (Ex. 14:16). In Joshua's first battle against the Amalekites, he was victorious so long as Moses held up his hands with his staff (Ex. 17:8-16). This was simply a symbol God assigned to show that the result was occurring by the power of God through the appointed leader.

In this case, when the men in ambush saw Joshua stretch forth his spear, they left their hiding places and ran into the city to set it on fire. Having done that, they left the city to attack the people of Ai from the rear. When the army that had been fleeing with Joshua saw the smoke of the city, they turned back to also attack the enemy. The men of Ai also saw the smoke of the city and realized what had happened. They were encircled by the enemy with nowhere to flee.

The result was that the soldiers of Ai were all slain except the king, who was brought to Joshua.

8:24-29 – Israel killed all the people of Ai, took the spoils for themselves, burned the city, and hanged the king of Ai.

Israel's victory was complete. They slew all the soldiers who came to fight against them. Then they entered the city and destroyed everyone there, men and women, as God had commanded. 12,000 people were slain in all.

We are told that Joshua did not draw back the hand with which he held the spear till all the people were consumed. This seems to have been a sign to the men of Israel to continue the attack (see on v18). It was similar to Moses' holding up his hands in the battle against Amalek (see reference above), but in that case Moses' hands also determined who prevailed in the battle.

The people then took the spoils of the city for themselves, just as God had said they could (see v2). The city itself was burned and made a desolate heap. This continued even till the time the book was written.

The king of Ai was captured in the battle and hung on a tree. At evening Joshua commanded the king's body to be taken down as taught in Deuteronomy 21:22,23. It was then cast into the entrance gate of the city and covered with a great heap of stones. That heap also remained until the time the book was written.

Nothing more is said about further battles in the central part of Canaan, though presumably there were others. Jericho and Ai must have been the major battles. After that whatever opposition Israel faced must have been relatively little, so we are told nothing about it.

8:30-35 - An Altar Built and the Law Read

8:30-32 – Joshua built an altar on Mount Ebal and offered sacrifices to God. Then he wrote on the stones a copy of the law of Moses.

The story then describes a period of worship and study of the law that Israel conducted at two mountains in central Canaan: Mt. Ebal and Mt. Gerizim. These are twin peaks found near Shechem (see **map**). This was the place where God promised Abraham that

He would give him the land of Canaan. Abraham had built an altar there (Gen. 12:6,7). Since the Israelites had now entered the land in fulfillment of the promise God made to Abraham at Shechem, it was appropriate for God to choose this as the place for the people to spend a special time of worship.

While Israel had still been east of Jordan, God had commanded Moses what to do to remind the people of God's law. See Deut. 27:1-13.

First they were to build an altar on Mt. Ebal made of whole stones that had not been engraved by man with any tool. See Deut. 27:2-8 (compare Ex. 20:25). They were to offer sacrifices to God on the altar, and they were to plaster the stones with plaster and write God's law on them. This is what Joshua had the people do as recorded here, exactly as Moses had commanded them.

No doubt this was to remind the people of God's law, and to impress deeply on their minds that God had given them this land. Since it was given them by God's blessing, they should serve Him faithfully in the land.

8:33-35 – Half the people stood at Mount Gerizim and half at Mount Ebal. There they read the words of the law including the blessings and the cursings.

Moses had commanded them to read the blessings and the curses after they entered the land. Six tribes were named who should stand on Mt. Gerizim to receive the record of the blessing and six were to stand on Mt. Ebal to receive the record of the curses. See Deut. 11:26-32; 27:11-14.

The blessing was the record of God's goodness that He would bring on the people if they would serve Him faithfully. See Deut. 28:1-14. The curse was the record of God's punishments that He would bring on the land if they did not serve Him. See Deut. 27:15-26; 28:15-68.

This is what Joshua read to the people here, exactly as Moses had commanded. Furthermore, the whole law was read to the people, with no exceptions. The assembly that heard this was all the people, including men, women, children, and strangers among them. All were to hear the whole law read.

Note that the people had been given the land because God had promised it to their fathers (Abraham, Isaac, Jacob, etc.). But whether or not they remained in the land would depend on the nation itself, whether or not they were faithful to God's covenant. This was made clear in the law that was read to them, even in the blessings and the curse. See Deut. 4:25-27,40; 5:33; 28:36,37;

29:22-28. They were reminded of this even as they were taking possession of the land.

Joshua 9

Alliance with Gibeonites – Joshua 9

9:1,2 – The inhabitants of Canaan formed alliances against Israel.

This story begins by describing a plan determined by the inhabitants of Canaan. They decided that they would gather together to fight against Israel. There is strength in unity. Israel had proved they could defeat individual cities, so other people united to fight them.

This may not refer to any one specific alliance but simply to a general plan that the peoples of the land decided to follow. There was no war with the people of some of these areas till considerably later. This would indicate that this was just a general plan.

This story appears to be then set aside for a while as the account tells about the alliance Joshua made with the Gibeonites.

9:3-6 – The Gibeonites sent ambassadors who pretended to have come a long distance to make an alliance with Israel.

Gibeon was a city actually located just southwest of Ai and north of Jerusalem (see **map**). It was not an insignificant city, but was a great city with many great warriors (10:2) among the Hivites (9:7). Verse 17 shows that the Gibeonite people actually inhabited a group of four cities in that area. So these people really lived quite close to the location of Israel's great victories. These people had heard of the victories of Israel and knew they were among Israel's next victims. They realized they were powerless to defend themselves, so they decided to work by deceit.

They pretended they were messengers sent from a distant country. They put on old patched clothes and sandals, carried old sacks, old food, and old wineskins. They came while Israel was still camped in Gilgal. There they asked Israel to make a peace treaty with them. They knew Israel would destroy anyone who lived in the land, so they pretended to be from a far country so Israel would make peace with them. Then they would try to hold Israel to their agreement.

The Waldrons hold the view that this Gilgal is not the one in the Jordan lowlands where Israel camped when they first crossed into Israel. They claim that Israel would have moved further into the land by this time. So this Gilgal would be one higher in the mountains.

9:7-13 – When Israel questioned them, the Gibeonites lied and said they had come from a far country.

Joshua and the people were suspicious of the Gibeonites, thinking they might actually be of the land of Canaan, in which case Israel should defeat them.

God had commanded them not to make covenants with the people of the land (Deut. 7:1-6,16; 9:1-5; 20:10-18; Ex. 23:31-33; 34:11,12). Note especially Deuteronomy 20:10-18, which expressly allowed Israel to make covenants with people who lived far from Canaan. But God had commanded Israel to destroy people who lived in the land. So they wanted to make sure these people were not of the land.

But the Gibeonites continued their lie. They said they were from a far country and there they had heard of Israel's great victories against the nations east of the Jordan. They claimed to have heard of the God Israel worshipped, and they wanted to join in alliance with Israel.

They used their old clothes and provisions as proof. They said their elders had told them to take these with them and they were all new when they left home. But in the great travel and long time that had passed, these had become old.

Of course, Israel should have suspected that such would not necessarily be true. But they were new at making war and dealing with crafty enemies. Their greatest error is yet to be described in the following verses.

9:14-17 – Israel made a covenant but failed to ask counsel of the Lord, then they later learned the truth.

Israel then made a covenant of peace with them, even swearing to them that they would not kill them. But we are told that they did not ask counsel of the Lord. This was a terrible mistake. God had specifically instructed that Joshua should seek guidance from the high priest – Numbers 27:21.

Study Notes on Joshua and Ruth

Israel may have made this kind of mistake at their first attack of Ai. But in this case there can be no doubt, for we are plainly told that they did not consult the Lord. Had they done so, He would no doubt have told them the truth, then He could have instructed them to destroy the Gibeonites or whatever course He chose.

Three days after making the covenant, however, Israel learned the truth. They heard that these people actually lived quite nearby. So Israel continued their journey and came to the cities where these people lived. They included Gibeon, Chephirah, Beeroth, and Kirjath Jearim (see **map**).

Imagine Israel's anger and shame at having accepted such deceit!

9:18-21 – Israel decided to honor the treaty, but to make the Gibeonites slaves.

Having learned of the Gibeonites deceit, Israel still determined not to harm them but to honor their treaty. The congregation complained against the rulers about the matter, but the rulers explained that they had made an oath in the name of God. They concluded that they could not hurt the Gibeonites because of that oath, lest wrath come upon them.

Nevertheless, they determined they would make the Gibeonites serve as slaves. They would be woodcutters and water carriers for all the congregation. The Gibeonites had offered to be Israel's servants (verse 11). Israel had promised not to kill them, but Gibeon offered to be servants, so that's what was done.

9:22-27 – Joshua then confronted Gibeon for their deceit and informed them that they must work as servants.

Joshua then called the Gibeonites and asked why they had deceived Israel saying they were from far away when actually they lived very close. Gibeon explained, as already discussed, that they knew God had promised to give Israel the land and had commanded them to kill everyone in the land. They feared for their lives, so they plotted this deceit.

Joshua then explained to the Gibeonites that they would be Israel's slaves, as the rulers had decided. They would be woodcutters and water carriers for the house of God (verse 23), for the altar in the place God would choose (verse 27). This appears to mean they would perform these tasks for the priests and Levites at the tabernacle and later the temple.

Gibeon agreed to this arrangement. They had offered to be servants; so this was what was done, and in this way the Gibeonites' lives were spared. At the time the book was written, the Gibeonites still served in that capacity.

Later information about the Gibeonites

After Saul became king, in his zeal for destroying Israel's enemies, he attempted to slay the Gibeonites – 2 Samuel 21:1-9. Because this was a violation of Israel's oath with the Gibeonites in Joshua's day, Israel suffered later during David's rulership. When David inquired of God about this, God explained this was because of Saul's attempt to kill the Gibeonites. Seven of Saul's offspring were then given to the Gibeonites to kill as punishment for Saul's sin.

Later references show that for many generations the tabernacle and/or a place of worship was located at Gibeon (1 Kings 3:4; 1 Chron. 16:39). Later, a group called the Nethinim was still working as servants to those who worked in the tabernacle and the temple. It is believed that these were the Gibeonites. See 1 Chronicles 9:2; Ezra 2:43,58; Nehemiah 10:28.

Why was this covenant binding?

The above passages, especially the case of Saul, demonstrate that God enforced the oath Israel had made to Gibeon. Even though the Gibeonites had lied and deceived, and even though He had commanded Israel to make no covenants with the people of the land, God upheld this covenant and punished Saul for not keeping it!

I have serious difficulties understanding why an oath made under these circumstances was binding. First, the oath was unknowingly a violation of God's law, and second it was made only because of false pretenses and lies from the Gibeonites. Why should they be rewarded for their lie by granting them protection? Why should Israel be allowed to continue in violation of God's law under such circumstances? I honestly cannot answer, yet clearly God did hold them to the oath.

Some things to consider are:

1) Israel had failed to consult God before making the oath. Perhaps keeping the oath served as a punishment to them for their failure to consult God. See Exodus 34:12.

2) Gibeon did appear to have faith in God. They clearly believed God would empower Israel to defeat them, regardless of any effort on their part. And they appear later to have served faithfully in the tabernacle and temple. God had said to kill the inhabitants so they would not lead Israel into idolatry. Clearly, the Gibeonites did not lead Israel into idolatry. Perhaps their faith made them an exception

to the rule that the people of the land should be slain, even as Rahab's faith had made her an exception.

3) The oath Israel made was not just to the Gibeonites but also before God. Such an oath was bound, not just by the people, but by God himself. This was the specific reason offered by the leaders of Israel why they had to keep the oath.

Could it be that, had Israel simply made a promise to Gibeon but then found out that the Gibeonites had lied, Israel could have freed themselves from the oath to Gibeon? But having made the oath before God, and knowing God was faithful not deceitful, perhaps that is why they had to keep it.

Israel had a means to know for sure if the people of Gibeon were telling the truth. They should have directly consulted God through the high priest, but they failed. We have no such means of direct communication today, but must study and apply the written word. We have no inspired way to know the facts about current circumstances, so could it be that the conclusion would be different today than in their case?

Lessons to consider:

1) Always be sure we consult God's will before making any commitment. Be sure the commitment is in harmony with God's will.

2) Do not lightly enter into any commitment, but especially commitments made to God.

3) Check out the commitment carefully to be sure what you are getting into before making it.

4) Attach conditions to any commitment such that, if it turns out that the information on which you have based the commitment is untrue, then you are free from the commitment.

These principles are especially important for commitments of major importance and long duration, such as marriage, etc.

Joshua 10

Southern Conquest – Joshua 10

10:1-27 - Defeat of the Alliance of Five Kings

10:1-4 – Adoni-Zedek, king of Jerusalem, led an alliance of southern kings to attack Gibeon for having made peace with Israel.

The king of Jerusalem was named Adoni-Zedek. He heard how Israel had defeated Jericho and Ai, then Gibeon had made peace with Israel. This caused him great fear. Not only had Jericho and Ai been defeated, but Gibeon was a great city, greater than Ai, having many valiant soldiers. Yet they had surrendered without a fight. Jerusalem was sure to be one of the next cities Israel attacked (see **map**).

So, Adoni-Zedek sought to make an alliance with the kings of other cities near him: Hoham king of Hebron, Piram king of Jarmuth, Japhia king of Lachish, and Debir king of Eglon (see **map**). Hebron was due south of Jerusalem, and Jarmuth was southwest but fairly close. Lachish and Eglon were further away to the west and southwest. This would make an alliance of five kings. This plan of making alliances had been decided on according to 9:1,2.

Since each of these cities had a king, it is clear that these kings were not rulers of great nations as we might think of kings today. The cities were apparently independent from one another, but each had its own king. They might usually act separately, but when faced with a common foe they would join forces for mutual protection as in this case.

The plan of this alliance, however, was not to attack Israel but to attack Gibeon for having made a treaty with Israel! We are not

Study Notes on Joshua and Ruth

told their reasoning behind this idea. On the one hand it would appear to be a mistake, since they would be turning their forces against other Canaanites instead of fighting Israel. Why waste their resources fighting those who were not the invaders? Perhaps they thought that Gibeon would fight with Israel against the Canaanites, so they made a preemptive strike. Perhaps they reasoned that attacking Gibeon would force them to break their treaty and join the Canaanites in fighting Israel. Or at least it might prevent other cities from making peace with Israel.

10:5-8 – When Gibeon appealed to Joshua for protection, God promised that Israel could defeat the alliance.

So as agreed, these five kings brought their armies to fight against Gibeon. But the men of Gibeon explained to Joshua what was happening and appealed to him to protect them. Joshua brought his army from Gilgal to fight.

One wonders why Joshua would do this. He had agreed not to kill the Gibeonites, but if the Canaanites killed them that would eliminate the Gibeonites. The oath had been made under circumstances of deceit and lying by Gibeon, so why were the Israelites bound to defend them? Perhaps that was part of the agreement. Perhaps they had agreed, not just to not harm them themselves, but to protect them from others. Yet I wonder why they would make such an agreement regarding people whom they believed to be far away from them.

On the other hand, perhaps Joshua went because he thought this would be a good time to attack the Canaanite kings. He may have correctly concluded that they would not be expecting Israel to attack. They would be fighting with Gibeon and would not be prepared for an attack at the same time from Israel. In any case this is what Joshua decided to do.

And apparently God agreed with this plan, for He offered His blessing on it. He promised Joshua that Israel would be able to defeat this army. It could not stand before them, but God had delivered them to Israel. Note that in this case Joshua apparently did consult God before attacking.

10:9-11 – The kings of the alliance fled before Israel and God attacked them with great hailstones.

Joshua added another element of surprise. He marched Israel all night in order to arrive at the battle before the kings were expecting them. They were able to take the Canaanite armies by surprise.

The result was a great slaughter of the Canaanites at Gibeon, so the Canaanite armies fled. Israel chased them down the road to Beth Horon as far as Azekah and Makkedah (see **map**). A town named Beth Horon is located west and a little north not far from Gibeon. Azekah and Makkedah are southwest and some distance from Gibeon. Perhaps there is another Beth Horon southwest of Gibeon. Or perhaps the road to Beth Horon leads west down the hillsides then splits or joins another road. So the Canaanites began fleeing west down the road to Beth Horon then turn and fled south. Or perhaps the armies simply separated and went separate directions.

God also worked with the Israelite armies. He caused great hailstones to fall on the Canaanites, so that more of them died from the hailstones than from Israel's soldiers.

10:12-14 – God heeded the prayer of Joshua for the sun and moon to stand still to lengthen the day.

As Israel was victorious, Joshua did not want their enemies to escape. If night came, the enemies might successfully scatter and find hiding places. So Joshua called upon God to stop the progress of time. He prayed for the sun to stand still over Gibeon as at high noon, and the moon to stand still in the valley of Aijalon. The Aijalon was a valley extending from Gibeon west and north to the plain of Sharon.

The point is that the earth would in effect stop spinning on its axis. This would stop the progress of time. The account says that this continued for a whole day. The sun stood still in the heavens and did not go down. In other words, the one day was lengthened till it took the duration of an additional day – two days' time, but the sun and moon moved only as much as in one day. This enabled Israel to take vengeance on the Canaanites.

Clearly this was miraculous. The account says nothing like it ever happened before or since. The Lord heeded Joshua's request, because He fought for Israel. This was impossible by natural law, yet it happened by the supernatural power of God. If the earth spun on its axis, then the day would not be extended. But if it did not spin, many other things would go wrong. Clearly, God suspended natural law to produce the needed result.

Note the description of the power of prayer, for it says that God heeded the voice of a man.

This event appears to be referred to also in Habakkuk 3:11. It is also said to be recorded in the book of Jasher. This book is also referred to in 2 Samuel 1:18. We are not told exactly what book this is. It is apparently not included in the Bible, therefore God saw fit

Study Notes on Joshua and Ruth

not to have it preserved for us today. Like other books sometimes referred to, it may have been an uninspired record which simply confirms the Bible record. Or it may have been inspired but was not needed since it simply duplicated what is contained in these other inspired books. In any case, whatever it contained, it is not necessary to our salvation. If it was necessary, God would have seen to it that it was preserved.

See Psalm 119:152,160; Isaiah 40:8; 30:8; John 12:48; 2 John 2; 1 Peter 1:23-25; 2 Peter 1:12-15; 2 Timothy 3:16,17.

10:15-20 – The five kings hid in a cave. Joshua had the entrance closed with stones till the Israelites completed their victory over the enemy armies.

Joshua and Israel returned to their camp at Gilgal. But the kings of the five cities hid themselves in a cave near Makkedah (see **map** and notes above). This was told to Joshua, but he did not want to take the time to deal with these kings yet. He told his soldiers to simply place large stones over the cave opening and place guards there, so the kings could not escape. Then his men were to continue pursuing the Canaanite armies to destroy as many as they could before the enemy escaped to fortified cities.

I'm not quite sure the significance of Israel's return to Gilgal. They had left it suddenly when they heard of the attack on Gibeon. Perhaps they returned for supplies or for the rest of the people or perhaps even for a brief rest after their all night march and two days of fighting. In any case, they did not stay long but continued the pursuit of the fleeing armies. We next find Israel camped at Makkedah – verse 21.

The result was a great victory for Israel. A great number of Canaanites were slaughtered, till finally some escaped to enter fortified cities. Apparently the meaning here is that Joshua knew they would seek to return to fortified cities, and some finally managed to do so. But he wanted as many killed as possible before they escaped.

10:21-27 – Joshua then had the five kings brought from the cave, Israelite leaders placed their feet on the necks of the kings, then the kings were hung.

Israel then camped at Makkedah, where the five kings had hidden in the cave. Israel arrived there safely. Their enemies had been so defeated and scattered that no one attacked Israel or attempted to hinder their movement.

At Makkedah the people went to the cave where the kings were hiding and brought them out. Joshua then called the leaders of the

Israelite army to place their feet on the necks of these kings. This represented the complete defeat of these kings and their subjugation to Israel. Joshua said that the Israelites should be strong and courageous in the continued battles ahead, because God would give them victory over all their other enemies, just as he had with these five kings.

The five kings were then hung on five trees. Their bodies were left there till sundown, then they were removed and thrown back in the cave. The opening to the cave was then covered again with rocks. The rocks and cave remained there even when this book was written. Clearly this would be another memorial to Israel's great victory.

10:28-43 - Capture of All of Southern Canaan

The rest of the chapter simply lists city after city in southern Canaan as Israel defeated them one by one. The pattern was consistently the same. Israel would attack a city and defeat it. The people there would be utterly destroyed, including the king (if any). Apparently, the defeat of the five-king alliance so demoralized the other cities that only few and minor attempts were made to form further alliances. Israel was able to simply go from one to another capturing them.

See a *map* for the location of the various cities.

10:28-39 – The cities captured

Makkedah

The five kings had been in a cave near Makkedah. Israel then proceeded to Makkedah and captured it, killing the king and all the people. Makkedah was west and somewhat south from Jerusalem.

Libnah

Libnah was a short distance southwest from Makkedah. Israel captured it and killed all its people and its king.

Lachish

Lachish had been one of the cities that had joined the five-king alliance. Their king and army had already been defeated, but here the city itself was captured and the remaining people were slain. Lachish was further south from Libnah.

Gezer

As Israel fought Lachish, Horam king of Gezer came to help defend them. This minor attempt at an alliance was also defeated. The king of Gezer and all his people were also slain. Gezer was located a considerable distance north of Lachish, north even of Makkedah.

Eglon

The next city attacked was Eglon. This city too had joined the five-king alliance. They were attacked and that city taken and all the people slain. Eglon was west and somewhat south from Lachish.

Hebron

Next came Hebron, another city from the five-king alliance. Israel attacked it, captured it, and killed all its people and its king. Apparently by this time they had appointed another king to replace the one Israel had killed at Makkedah. Hebron was a significant distance east from Eglon.

Debir

The last city specifically named is Debir. Israel also attacked it, captured it, and killed all its people. Debir was located west and somewhat south from Hebron.

No doubt other smaller cities were captured along the way. The ones named were surely the largest and most significant ones. But in the process Israel took all the land. Verse 37 even states that, in the capture of Hebron other cities were also captured.

10:40-43 – In this way, Israel completely captured the cities and peoples of the southern areas of Canaan.

This completed Israel's defeat of the Canaanites in the southern regions. They had conquered all the mountain, lowland, and wilderness areas in the south, utterly slaying all the people. As a result, Israel had captured all the land from Kadesh Barnea to Gaza and the area of Goshen as far as Gibeon. All their kings were defeated and all their territory captured by the power of God fighting for Israel.

Kadesh Barnea was located very far south, a great distance from any city named thus far. This is the place Israel had camped many years previously when they sent the 12 spies into the land and then refused to enter (Numbers 13). The great distances involved here show that other cities were also defeated; but by defeating the main cities, Israel took control of the whole area.

Gaza was located at the Mediterranean Sea west from the Dead Sea. The only Goshen I know was the area in Egypt where Israel had lived during Joseph's rule. This is not likely the place referred to here; presumably it is an area in Canaan. The Waldrons say Goshen was an area in southern Judah. Gibeon, of course, was the city where this great series of battles had begun.

Having captured all this territory, Joshua and Israel returned to their camp at Gilgal.

The Waldrons point out that some of these same cities are said to be captured in Judges (1:10-12). If Israel captured them all in Joshua's day, no doubt they did not leave people to populate and defend them. The dividing of the land came later. So perhaps people from surrounding territories returned to these cities to repopulate them, so they had to be taken again later. Or the Waldrons suggest that perhaps not all these cities were actually taken at this exact point in the record but that eventually they were captured. In that case, this chapter would be a summary of the victories, but not necessarily an exact chronological record.

Joshua 11

Northern Conquest – Joshua 11

11:1-3 – *Jabin, king of Hazor, formed an alliance of northern kings against Israel.*

The southern alliance against Israel had failed. The inhabitants living in the north surely knew they were next. They had only three choices: (1) they could attempt to make peace with Israel, which would not work because God had forbidden it; (2) they could wait for Israel to attack them one by one; or (3) they could join an alliance so Israel would have to fight them together. They chose the latter approach as the only sensible one.

This alliance was initiated by Jabin king of Hazor. He sought to form an alliance with Jobab king of Madon, the king of Shimron, and the king of Achshaph. See a ***map*** for the location of these cities. Hazor is located in the far north near the Jordan River north of the Sea of Galilee (Chinneroth). Madon is thought to have been located just west of the Sea of Galilee. Achshaph was probably further west from Madon, considerably closer to the Mediterranean, and Shimron was south from Achshaph.

Also invited to the alliance were other kings from the north, in the mountains, in the plain south of the Sea of Chinneroth (Galilee), in the lowland, and in the heights of Dor. Dor was located on the Mediterranean west of the lower end of the Sea of Galilee.

Also included were Canaanites in the east and in the west, the Amorite, the Hittite, the Perizzite, the Jebusite in the mountains, and the Hivite below Hermon in the land of Mizpah. Hermon was a great mountain at the extreme north of the land where the Jordan River began. Mizpah sounds to be an area near Hermon, but I am unable to determine its exact location.

This was a huge alliance including great numbers of soldiers from many different lands. One would think the Israelites were clearly outnumbered.

11:4,5 – These kings gathered at the waters of Merom with innumerable soldiers, horses, and chariots.

All these inhabitants from all these areas met to fight against Israel. Their number was so great that they were like sand by the seashore – in other words, they could not be counted. They had many horses and chariots. These would be a great advantage in strength and mobility in fighting in those days. We have no indication that Israel had either horses or chariots.

It would appear that Israel was so greatly outnumbered that their defeat would be inevitable. But such large aggregates of armies often have difficulty working together. They may be numerous, but are hard to coordinate into a working unit. More important, Israel had God on their side.

These kings and their armies assembled at the waters of Merom to make a camp in preparation for the battle against Israel. Merom was just southwest of Hazor, still considerably north of the Sea of Galilee (see **map**). Meeting here would have required a long march for Israel.

11:6-9 – With God's assurance of victory, Joshua attacked, defeated them, hamstrung their horses, and burned their chariots.

God again assured Joshua that Israel would be victorious. Despite the incredibly large number of enemies and their horses, God assured Joshua not to be afraid. God said the enemy would all be slain before Israel the next day. Israel should hamstring their horses and burn their chariots. To hamstring a horse was to partially disable it, making it unsuitable for use in warfare but still suitable for use in farming.

So, at God's assurance, Joshua led Israel to attack the next day suddenly, when apparently the enemy was not prepared. Few details are given of this battle, but Israel was completely victorious. The enemy fled to Greater Sidon, to the Brook Misrephoth, and to the Valley of Mizpah eastward. All of the enemy was killed, and Israel hamstrung their horses and burned their chariots as God had said.

Sidon was an ancient city far up the coast of the Mediterranean Sea. Greater Sidon may mean the general area around that city. The Brook Misrephoth refers to an area on the Mediterranean almost due west from Merom (see **map**). Again Mispah is unknown.

Study Notes on Joshua and Ruth

11:10-15 — Joshua destroyed all the inhabitants of the cities, burned Hazor, and took much spoils.

Having defeated the coalition of armies, Israel then proceeded to take the cities of the area as they had in the south. They began with Hazor, the city of king Jabin who had led the alliance against Israel. They killed the king and all the people of the city, leaving no survivors, and burned the city. Hazor was later rebuilt (see Judges 4:2; 1 Kings 9:15).

Joshua then led Israel to capture the other cities in the area, killing their kings and all their inhabitants. They took the spoils for themselves, including the livestock, but they killed all the people. In doing this, they obeyed God's command to them through Moses, exactly as God wanted, leaving nothing undone.

We are told that, except for Hazor, they did not burn the cities that stood on mounds. Cities in that day were often built on mounds, so they were harder for defenders to attack. Also as centuries passed, people tended to build their cities higher and higher.

It seems that Israel burned only the most offending of cities, leaving the others for their own future occupation. This had the disadvantage, however of leaving the cities temporarily uninhabited. Perhaps this explains why some of them had to be recaptured later, as inhabitants from surrounding areas moved back in after Israel had left.

11:16-20 — Joshua made war a long time completing the capture of the land.

This was the end of the major battles Israel needed to fight. They had overcome the greatest armies from the greatest cities. This was followed by a long period of war against the surrounding cities and their kings. We are told few specifics, since apparently the ensuing battles were not sufficiently important for us to be given details.

We are also not told exactly how long this took. Calculations based on Joshua 14:7-10 would imply that altogether the capture of the land took six or seven years.

The result was that Israel captured and killed all the kings of the area, the mountain country, all the South, all the land of Goshen, the lowland, and the Jordan plain, the mountains of Israel and its lowlands. This included from Mount Halak and the ascent to Seir, even as far as Baal Gad in the Valley of Lebanon below Mount Hermon.

Many of these are general areas. The Waldrons say Goshen was an area in southern Judah. Hymel says Mt. Halak was south of

Beersheeba, and Baal-Gad was at the foot of Mt. Hermon. Seir was Edom to the south of the Dead Sea and Mt. Hermon was a mountain far north of the Sea of Galilee. The point is that this is a very broad area including essentially all of the land of Canaan. This would take a long time.

Of all the cities and people in the land, the only one that made a covenant with Israel was Gibeon, and they had done so by deceit. All the other people fought against Israel and were destroyed. The account says they fought because God moved them to fight. He had determined to destroy them as He had commanded Moses, so He moved them to fight against Israel. Again, this was not cruelty on God's part, but justice. These people were so abominably corrupt that they deserved destruction.

11:21-23 – Joshua also slew the Anakim. He captured all the territory that God had promised through Moses that He would give.

The account ends with the destruction of the Anakim. These were fierce fighters, many of them giants. They lived in the mountains around Hebron, Debir, Anab and the mountains of Judah and Israel. Hebron was an area captured in chapter 10, a city just west of the Dead Sea. Debir was southwest from Hebron and had also been captured in 10:38,39. Anab was a short distance south of Debir. (See **map**.)

The account states that Anakim were scattered throughout the region, but they were all destroyed, leaving none in the land of Israel. They remained only in Gaza, Gath, and Ashdod, areas where we will later see that the Philistines maintained control. They are located relatively near the Mediterranean Sea.

This may not necessarily mean that this was done following the war with the northern alliance, since many of these lived in areas previously captured. Rather it appears to be a summary of how the Anakim had been defeated throughout this period of war.

The Anakim were such large, fierce fighters that the sight of them had unnerved the ten tribes the first time Israel had approached Canaan to capture it (Num. 13:28,33; Deut. 1:28; 2:10,11,21). Perhaps this is why here we are told that Israel successfully overwhelmed and defeated them. We will read more about them in Joshua chapters 14,15. One wonders if Goliath and similar giants later were descendants of these people, since they came from the areas of the Philistines where the Anakim were left.

Note that, as early as the writings of Joshua, a distinction is made between Judah and Israel (verse 21). They were not separate nations by any means, but they identified different regions that

Study Notes on Joshua and Ruth

finally resulted in different nations many years later in the reign of the kings.

The account of battles ends by telling us that Israel had completed their task of taking the land. They captured it all as God had commanded them through Moses. Joshua gave it to the tribes for their inheritance, and the land had peace from war. This is a summary statement, since the land had not yet been divided to the tribes.

Joshua 12

List of Kings Defeated – Joshua 12

This chapter simply lists the kings defeated by the Israelites, including the cities or territories they ruled.

Sihon king of Heshbon

First, the kings east of Jordan are listed. Sihon, king of the Amorites, lived in Heshbon (see ***map***). He ruled half of Gilead, from Aroer on the Arnon to the river Jabbok. He apparently also controlled territory in the Jordan plain from the Sea of Chinnereth (Galilee) to the Dead Sea.

This territory had been captured by Israel under Moses' leadership.

Og, king of Bashan

Moses also led Israel to defeat Og, king of Bashan. He also ruled half of Gilead in the north, from the territory of Sihon to Mt. Hermon north of the Sea of Galilee.

All this territory east of Jordan was captured under Moses' leadership and given to the tribes of Reuben, Gad, and half of Manasseh.

Territory west of Jordan captured under Joshua.

The territory west of the Jordan was captured under the leadership of Joshua, as described in this book to this point. The kings defeated are listed as a summary here. The territory included from the Valley of Lebanon all the way to hills near Seir (Edom).

Altogether 31 kings were defeated.

Study Notes on Joshua and Ruth

Part 3. Israel Divides Canaan (Joshua 13-24)

Joshua 13

Division of the Land among the Tribes – Joshua 13-22

Joshua 13 - Inheritance of the Tribes East of Jordan

13:1-6 – Joshua was growing older, and there were many areas of Canaan yet to be possessed. But God commanded him to divide the land among the tribes.

Israel had conquered the land, but Joshua was growing old and the land had not yet been divided among the tribes. God spoke to Joshua, described the land, and commanded him to divide it by lot among the tribes as God had commanded.

It appears that not all the inhabitants of the land had even yet been driven out. Surely the Israelites had not yet moved into their territories. Yet God had Joshua divide the territories up to the tribes based on their faith that God would yet drive out the inhabitants before them.

13:7-14 – The land east of Jordan had been conquered under the leadership of Moses and divided among the 2½ tribes.

The land west of Jordan was to be divided among 9 ½ of the tribes, because the territory east of Jordan had been given to the 2 ½ tribes of Reuben, Gad, and half of Manasseh. This included the territories captured from Sihon king of Heshbon and Og king of Bashan. This territory is here described, naming cities and areas included.

The Geshurites and Maachathites had not been driven out from among Israel but remained in their territories even when this was written.

This land east of Jordan had not only been captured but had been divided among the 2 ½ tribes. However, the Levites did not inherit land as a tribe. They were given individual cities scattered throughout the territories of the other tribes. This was because their inheritance was the service they did to God among the tribes.

13:15-23 – Reuben was given much of the territory that had been controlled by Sihon, king of Heshbon.

Reuben's inheritance is described, naming cities and boundaries. As the inheritance of each tribe is described in the following chapters, the territories are difficult to know exactly today, though of course it was clear to the Israelites when it occurred.

In general, their inheritance included territory taken from Sihon king of Heshbon. It stretched from the Arnon river north along the Dead Sea till it reached the Jordan River. See **map**.

The record tells again that the Israelites had slain Balaam, son of Beor, who had been hired by Balak to prophesy against Israel. See Numbers 22-25.

13:24-28 – Gad inherited north of Reuben, including the rest of the territory captured from Sihon.

Gad's inheritance is described. It was the territory north of Reuben, including the rest of the region captured from Sihon king of Heshbon. It included much of the land of Gilead along the Jordan River as far north as the Sea of Galilee (Chinnereth). See **map**.

13:29-33 – The half tribe of Manasseh inherited the territory captured from Og king of Bashan.

The half tribe of Manasseh also inherited east of Jordan. Their inheritance was generally the territory captured from Og king of Bashan. This was north of Gad's inheritance, including the rest of Gilead. See **map**.

Again we are told that Levi did not receive a territory, since they received cities scattered throughout the land.

We might wonder why God had the borders of each of these territories recorded in Scripture. We today would find great difficulty in determining the exact borders of each of the territories. And Israel was long ago removed from the land and taken into

Study Notes on Joshua and Ruth

captivity. Today, the borders of their territories in Canaan is of no significance whatever under the gospel.

However, the descriptions of the territories of the tribes would have been of great value to the people of Israel for many years after the time of Joshua. No doubt they understood the landmarks, cities, and borders that are described in the record. This would enable them to keep clear exactly what territory belonged to each tribe. Having a written record would settle any disputes, especially since the lots would have been determined by God Himself and recorded in Scripture by inspiration.

As with genealogies, these records also show us that these events were historic fact. By recording specific geographic landmarks, the Holy Spirit shows without doubt that these were real events that took place in real territories among real people.

Joshua 14

Joshua 14 - Inheritance of Caleb

14:1-5 — The territory west of Jordan was to be divided by lot among the remaining 9½ tribes.

The previous chapter recorded the area given to the 2 ½ tribes who inherited east of Jordan. Now begins the account of the remaining 9 ½ tribes that inherited west of Jordan. This inheritance was supervised by Joshua and the high priest Eleazar along with the heads of the various tribes.

The territory would be divided into 10 areas, then the areas would be assigned to the various tribes by lot, as God had instructed through Moses (Numbers 26:55). The Levites would not receive a territory, as discussed in the previous chapter. They received cities scattered throughout the territories of the other tribes, so they could lead in spiritual service (Numbers 35:2-8).

Since Levi did not receive a territory, one might expect that would leave a total of only eleven tribes to inherit territory. However, Joseph received the birthright, including a double portion of territory. This was accomplished, according to the instructions of Jacob, by giving a separate inheritance to each of Joseph's two sons Manasseh and Ephraim (verse 4). The effect was to make a total of 12 tribes to inherit, because Joseph's descendants counted as two tribes. See Genesis 48:1-22 (esp. verse 5); 1 Chronicles 5:1.

14:6-9 — Caleb requested the inheritance that had been promised to him by Moses.

Caleb was the son of Jephunneh of the tribe of Judah. He came to Joshua, along with other people of the tribe of Judah, to request that he be given the inheritance Moses had promised him. See Numbers 13,14.

When Israel had first approached Canaan at Kadesh Barnea, Moses had sent twelve spies into the land. Ten of them had brought back bad reports saying the people could not take the land. This had

Study Notes on Joshua and Ruth

discouraged the people, leading them to refuse to go into the land. As a result, God had said the older generation would not be allowed to enter at all, but would wander in the wilderness forty years till they died.

The other two spies, however, had maintained their faith in God and had urged the people to enter. Those two were Joshua and Caleb. God had said they would be the only two of the older generation to enter the land. Obviously, Joshua entered as Moses' successor and leader of the nation. Caleb also had entered, as God had promised, and now he was requesting to be given the inheritance promised him. See Numbers 14:23,24; Deuteronomy 1:36.

14:10-15 – Caleb was given Hebron as an inheritance.

Caleb had been 40 years old as a faithful spy at Kadesh Barnea (v7). Forty-five years had passed since then, making Caleb 85 years old. Yet he was still strong and active. He believed he could lead his people to capture the territory of his inheritance from the people of the land. So, he requested to be given a territory among the same region where he had traveled when he spied out the land.

The territory they had spied had been inhabited by the Anakim, the giants, as discussed in 11:21. These were the giants whose appearance had so discouraged the Israelites. One of the cities the Anakim had inhabited was Hebron, and that was the territory Joshua said Caleb could have. It had formerly been named Kirjath Arba, after Arba who was the greatest leader of the Anakim.

We are not told here, but chapter 15 records the actual taking of the city of Hebron by Caleb and his descendants (15:13ff). The chronology is somewhat confusing, however. Joshua 11:21 had said that Joshua had driven the Anakim out of Hebron when they had defeated the armies that attacked them. It is unclear whether that was a summary statement that included the later victory by Caleb.

Or perhaps the event recorded here in chapter 14 had actually occurred earlier, and Caleb had been the leader who actually won the victory in chapter 11. Or perhaps the best explanation is that the Anakim had been defeated and driven from Hebron earlier as recorded in chapter 11 but had returned afterward as Israel fought elsewhere. So now Caleb's family had to fight to defeat them again, but this time it did not require the whole army to win the victory.

The land is again said to have peace from war. The occasional battles to capture or re-capture various areas are apparently not viewed as an exception. The point is that the major warfare required to take the land was now over. There was no doubt in anyone's mind who now controlled the territory. It belonged to Israel and any future battles were simply to remove other people living in their territory. The war itself was over.

Joshua 15

Joshua 15 - The Inheritance of the Tribe of Judah

15:1-12 – The borders of Judah

As with the tribes east of Jordan, I will not attempt to give a technical description of Judah's territory. As before, in fact it is difficult to determine the exact location of many places named on the boundaries after so many years have passed.

In general, Judah's territory stretched from the Dead Sea on the east to the Mediterranean Sea on the west. The northern border stretched westward from the northern tip of the Dead Sea, where the Jordan entered the Sea. It passed Jerusalem and went west to the sea. On the south, Judah's territory stretched to Edom and the wilderness of Zin south of Canaan.

15:13-19 – Caleb captured his inheritance in Hebron, driving out three Anak warriors. Othniel married Caleb's daughter as a reward for capturing Debir.

As recorded in 14:6-15, Joshua had agreed that Caleb could receive Hebron as his inheritance. This had formerly been named Kirjath-Arba, after the great Anakim leader named Arba, father of Anak.

Caleb and his family were successful in capturing Hebron, driving out in the process three Anak warriors named Sheshai, Ahiman, and Talmai. This would be no small feat, since these men were giants and great warriors that had so frightened Israel's spies when they first came to Canaan. See notes on chapter 14. As discussed in chapter 14, the chronology here is not clear, but the most likely explanation is that Israel had earlier defeated Hebron driving out the Anakim, but more had returned and had to be driven out at this time by Caleb.

Caleb and his family then went to another nearby city named Kirjath Sepher. This was later renamed Debir. This city too was captured according to chapter 10:38,39. So again some people must have returned in the meanwhile.

Caleb offered to give his daughter Achsah as wife to whomever would attack and capture Debir. This challenge was taken up by Othniel, Caleb's nephew (son of Caleb's brother Kenaz). He attacked and captured Debir, so Caleb gave him his daughter Achsah as promised.

After the victory, Achsah and Othniel agreed to ask Caleb to also give them a field including springs for water. This request was made and Caleb agreed giving her upper and lower springs.

This event is also recorded in Judges 1:11-15. It is obviously the same story, so it cannot have happened both times. Perhaps the story occurred in Joshua's day as recorded in Joshua 15 but is included in Judges 1 for completeness to explain in some detail the victories of Judah and to introduce Othniel who later became a judge. (Or vice-versa, it may have occurred later as recorded in Judges 1, but for completeness it was recorded in the book of Joshua by the one who later wrote the story. But it would seem that would make Caleb a very old man here, since Joshua had already died.)

This same Othniel, Caleb's nephew, later became a judge of Israel as recorded in Judges 3:7-11.

15:20-63 – The cities given to Judah

The record then names the cities included in the territory given to Judah. Some of these had been named in the battles Israel fought in capturing the land. Others are named later in subsequent events in Israel's history.

Perhaps the most significant is that the people were not able to drive the Jebusites out of Jerusalem. Even at that time Jerusalem was a great stronghold. When the record was written, Jerusalem still had not been taken. It was later captured by David as recorded in m 2 Samuel 5:6-9.

Study Notes on Joshua and Ruth

Joshua 16

Joshua 16 - The Inheritance of the Tribe of Ephraim

16:1-4 – Joseph's sons next to inherit

The two tribes coming from Joseph were next to inherit. Again, we will not attempt to describe the territory specifically.

The southern boundary of their inheritance stretched from the Jordan at Jericho west past Bethel to the sea (see **map**).

16:5-10 – Inheritance of Ephraim

The territory of Ephraim went north from the southern border described above. Some of their cities were actually within the territory given to Manasseh (compare 17:8,9).

However, Canaanites continued to live in Gezer. Ephraim did not drive them out, as God had commanded them to do, but instead made them forced laborers. Already trouble was brewing as Israel disobeyed God's command to completely destroy all the people of the land.

Joshua 17

Joshua 17 - The Inheritance of Manasseh

17:1-6 – The daughters of Zelophehad requested to receive their inheritance as promised by Moses, since their father had no sons.

Half the tribe of Manasseh had already received their inheritance east of Jordan. That inheritance went to the descendants of Manasseh's firstborn Machir. This chapter records how the rest of the sons of Manasseh received their inheritance.

Zelophehad was a great grandson of Machir. He had no sons to inherit after him. God had arranged for his daughters to inherit in his place, as discussed in Numbers 27:1-11 and chapter. 36. Here these daughters came to Eleazar the high priest, Joshua, and the rulers to remind him about their inheritance.

The territory given to the descendants of Manasseh west of Jordan was then divided into ten sections, and the daughters of Zelophehad received their inheritance among the sons who inherited.

17:7-13 – The territory given to Manasseh

Like Ephraim's territory, Manasseh's extended from the Jordan westward, but Manasseh's territory was north of Ephraim's. The brook Kanah separated them. Manasseh's territory extended to the Mediterranean Sea on the west (see **map**).

On the north it extended to the plain of Jezreel at Megiddo. The tribes of Issachar and Asher were north of Manasseh. Again we are told that some towns inhabited by Ephraimites were actually in Manasseh's territory. Likewise, Manasseh was given some towns that were actually in the territories of Issachar and Asher.

And again, as with Ephraim, Manasseh was unable to drive out the Canaanites from some of the cities in their territory. When Manasseh was strong, they put the Canaanites to slave labor, but never drove them out completely.

Study Notes on Joshua and Ruth

17:14-18 – When the sons of Joseph complained that they did not have enough territory, Joshua said they should clear the forests and drive out the inhabitants.

Some people from the descendants of Joseph (Ephraim and Manasseh) later came to Joshua and complained about the amount of territory given them. They said they were a great people and should be given more territory. Actually, they had been given a very large territory right in the midst of the land, and in addition half of the tribe of Manasseh had land east of Jordan.

Joshua responded by pointing out that, if they were such a great people, then they should be able to make room for themselves within the territory given them. He suggested first that they should clear the forests in the territory they had and make room to live there.

The people complained that this was not enough room and they could not drive out the inhabitants in the valley of Jezreel because they were strong and had chariots made of iron. This begins to show the real problem. Israel lacked room because they had not destroyed all the people of the land!

Joshua replied that a great people, as they claimed to be, could handle this situation. He claimed they had been given more than one lot, but it was their duty to clear it of forest and Canaanites. Here the failure of the people to destroy all the people of the land was already becoming a problem. The people complained about lack of room, but they lacked room because they had not obeyed God and driven out all the people of the land.

Joshua 18

Joshua 18&19 - Division of the Land for Other Tribes

18:1-3 — The tabernacle was set up at Shiloh. The remaining seven tribes were admonished to choose their possession.

Israel met and set up the tabernacle at Shiloh. Shiloh was in the territory of Ephraim north of Jerusalem and even north from the city Israel had captured at Ai (see **map**). The tabernacle is mentioned later as being at Shiloh. Apparently it remained there for quite some time. See Judges 18:31; 21:19; 1 Sam. 1:3; 3:21; 14:3; Jer. 7:12; Psa. 78:60.

At this point five tribes had obtained the land of their inheritance: 2½ on the east side and 2½ on the west side. The remaining seven tribes needed to receive their inheritance and settle there. The land was subdued before Israel in the sense they clearly had control of it, but still the tribes needed to move into their inheritance.

Joshua called the people together and remonstrated against them for procrastinating. They were neglecting to possess the land God had given them.

18:4-10 — Men were sent to divide up the remaining land into seven parcels to be appointed by lot to the remaining tribes.

Joshua proposed that each of the tribes appoint three men to survey the land (this appears to me to refer to the seven tribes that remained to inherit territory, though perhaps it refers to all twelve tribes). This group would examine the land and divide it up into seven parcels of land. Then Joshua would cast lots to determine what territory would be given to which tribes.

The territories would not include the areas that had already been assigned to tribes east and west of Jordan. Nor would it

Study Notes on Joshua and Ruth

include any territory for the Levites, since they would inherit cities but not a territory.

As Joshua had instructed, the men traveled through the land writing down the cities. Then they divided up the area into seven territories. Then Joshua cast lots to determine which of these territories would be assigned to which tribes.

18: 11-28 – Territory assigned to Benjamin

The first tribe whose territory is then described was Benjamin. They received a region between what had been assigned to Judah and Ephraim. It bordered at the Jordan north of the Dead Sea and stretched to the west between Judah and Ephraim's territories.

Again, we will not attempt to determine specific boundaries, but this was the general area they received.

The account then names the cities given to Benjamin.

Joshua 19

19:1-9 – The inheritance of Simeon

The inheritance of the tribe of Simeon is described next. Their inheritance was taken out of the territory of the tribe of Judah, because the territory given to Judah was more than they needed. So Simeon was given a number of cities found in Judah's territory.

19:10-16 – The inheritance of Zebulun

The next territory described was given to the tribe of Zebulun. Again, we will not attempt to determine specific boundaries. However, in general Zebulun's territory was centrally located north of Manasseh's territory (the Manasseh west of Jordan). It was surrounded by Asher to the west, Issachar to the southeast, and Naphtali to the northeast.

19:17-23 – The inheritance of Issachar

Next came the territory given to Issachar. They received next to Zebulun, but southeast from them. Issachar held a region along the Jordan River, north of the valley of Jezreel but south of the Sea of Galilee. They were surrounded by Manasseh to the south, Zebulun to the northwest and Naphtali to the north.

19:24-31 – The inheritance of Asher

Asher's territory was along the Mediterranean Sea. It extended north from Manasseh and northwest from Mt. Carmel all along the sea as far north as the city of Tyre. It had Manasseh to its south, Zebulun to its southeast, and Naphtali to its east.

19:32-39 – The inheritance of Naphtali

Next came Naphtali. They inherited along the west coast of the Sea of Galilee and northward from there between the Jordan River to their east and Asher to their west. Issachar was to their south and Zebulun to their southwest.

19:40-48 – The inheritance of Dan

The last tribe to be given its territory was Dan. Dan received territory also extending to the Mediterranean Sea, but west of

Study Notes on Joshua and Ruth

Ephraim and Benjamin. They had Judah to their south and Manasseh to their north.

Later Dan also took some territory in the far north of Canaan along the Jordan River near Mt. Hermon. This was previously called Leshem, but people of Dan captured it. So their territory, like Manasseh's, was divided into two separate areas.

19:49-51 – Joshua was given as his inheritance Timnath Serah in Ephraim.

Caleb had been a faithful spy and was given his own special inheritance in Israel as one of the only two people from the older generation to enter Canaan. The same was true for Joshua, so he too was given his own inheritance. He was given a city named Timnath Serah in Ephraim (see **map**).

All these divisions of territory were agreed upon by the people under the leadership of Eleazar the priest and Joshua.

Joshua 20

Joshua 20 - Appointment of Cities of Refuge

20:1-6 – God commanded Joshua to appoint cities of refuge for the manslayer to flee for protection.

In Numbers 35 God had instructed Moses about the cities of refuge. They were to be cities where a manslayer could flee if he had accidentally killed another person. These cities are discussed further in Exodus 21:13; Numbers 35:22-25; Deuteronomy 19:1-13.

According to Numbers 35, if anyone accidentally killed another person, he could flee to the city of refuge. Eventually his case would be tried. If a person killed a man by striking him with an iron implement or with a stone or a wooden weapon in his hand, then he would be considered a murderer, and murderers must be put to death. The same would apply if he shoved the man because he hated him, or if he were to lie in wait and throw something at him and kill him. Or it would apply if he just struck the man with his hand because he hates him. All such cases were considered murder.

The avenger of blood would carry out the sentence of death. See Numbers 35:21,24,27; Deuteronomy 19:6,12. The avenger of blood was a near kinsman (see NKJV footnote). If he found the murderer outside the city of refuge, he could kill him.

On the other hand, suppose a man suddenly pushed a man without any hatred toward him, or suppose he threw something without lying in wait, or suppose he threw a stone without seeing the man, yet the man was not an enemy and there was no intent to harm. These cases were considered "accidental" (compare Exodus 21:12-14). The congregation must make a judgment in the case to determine whether or not the man was guilty of murder.

If the death was determined to be accidental, then the congregation should return him to the city of refuge to deliver or save him from death at the hand of the avenger of blood. He must remain in that city, not going outside the city limits till the death of the anointed high priest.

Study Notes on Joshua and Ruth

If the manslayer were to venture outside the city limits, and if the avenger of blood caught him there, the avenger could kill him without himself being guilty of murder. The manslayer would then be responsible for his own death, since he should have stayed in the city.

When the high priest died, however, the manslayer would be free to leave the city of refuge and return to his home without danger.

20:7-9 – The cities appointed

There were to be three cities on each side of the Jordan, a total of six altogether. They were scattered throughout the territory Israel held so that, no matter where a man killed another man, he could flee to a city that was relatively close. So three were on the west of Jordan and three on the east, spaced out across the land.

The three appointed on the west were Kedesh in Galilee in the mountains of Naphtali, Shechem in the mountains of Ephraim, and Kirjath Arba (Hebron) in the mountains of Judah. The three east of Jordan were assigned to Bezer in the tribe of Reuben, Ramoth in Gilead from the tribe of Gad, and Golan in Bashan from the tribe of Manasseh. (See **map**.)

Joshua 21

Joshua 21 - Cities Appointed for the Levites

21:1-3 – The Levites requested to receive the cities that were to be appointed to them.

All the tribes had received their lands of inheritance, and the cities of refuge had been appointed. One more group of people needed to receive their possession: the Levites. The heads of the Levite houses came before Eleazar and Joshua to request to be given the cities that God had commanded Moses to be given to them.

This was also discussed in Numbers 35. The Levites were not to inherit a territory as a tribe, as did other tribes. Instead, they were to receive cities scattered throughout the land. This was to include common land around each city.

The common lands would extend outward from the cities themselves. These lands were for the grazing of the Levites' herds, cattle, and all animals. The Levites were to be given 48 cities altogether, of which six would be cities of refuge where the manslayer could flee (as described in chapter 20).

Tribes with larger land holdings would be required to give a larger number of cities to the Levites, and tribes with smaller land holdings would give fewer cities.

21:4-8 – The number of cities assigned by family

The Levites were divided into three families according to the sons of Levi. The Kohathites, descendants of Kohath, included the descendants of Aaron who would include the priests. The descendants of Aaron were to be given thirteen cities in Judah, Simeon, and Benjamin. The other Kohathites were to be given ten cities in Ephraim, Dan, and the half tribe of Manasseh west of Jordan.

The descendants of Gershom, the Gershomites, were to be given 13 cities from Issachar, Asher, Naphtali, and from the half-tribe of Manasseh east of Jordan.

Study Notes on Joshua and Ruth

Then the descendants or Merari, the Merarites, were to be given 12 cities from Reuben, Gad, and Zebulun.

21:9-42 – The cities designated for the Levites

These verses name the 48 cities given to the Levites. Again, we will not try to specifically identify them and their location.

The only point of particular interest is the fact that Hebron was appointed a city for the Levites, but it had already been given to Caleb. The text explains that the city with its common lands was given to the Levites, but Caleb was given the fields around the city along with the villages that surrounded it.

21:43-45 – God gave Israel all the land that he had promised to their ancestors that He would give.

God had promised to Abraham, Isaac, and Jacob that he would make their descendants a great nation, give them the land of Canaan, and through their descendants would come a great blessing on all nations (salvation through Jesus) – see Genesis 12:2,3,7; 15:5-8,18-21; 13:15,17; 18:18; 22:17,18; 24:7; 26:3,4,24; 28:3,4; 32:12.

This passage of Joshua expressly states that God did fulfill that promise. See also 23:14; compare 11:23. Specifically, the account says that God gave Israel all the land that He had sworn to their fathers to give. They took possession of the land and dwelt in it.

In the land, He gave them rest. Their enemies could not withstand them, but the Lord delivered their enemies into their hands. Again, nothing failed of anything good that God had promised to do for Israel. It all came to pass. There is no disputing such plain language.

God gave them the land because of the promises He had made to their fathers. So the passage states. But their keeping the land depended on their own willingness to be faithful (see 23:11-16). They turned out not to be faithful, so they lost the land eventually. But for now they had it as God had promised.

Amazingly, there are those who say that Israel never received all the land God promised to give. So they claim this promise to Abraham must still be fulfilled sometime yet in the future. They also claim that God still has great blessings for the physical descendants of Israel. This plainly contradicts this passage and many others. It simply is a false claim, and as such it denies the accuracy of Scripture, specifically the accuracy of Joshua.

For further information, see our articles on premillennialism at our Bible Instruction web site at www.gospelway.com/instruct/.

At this point, God had fulfilled two of these three major promises to Abraham regarding his descendants. The people became a great nation in Egypt. That first promise was fulfilled by the time Moses led them out of Egypt. Now the second promise had been fulfilled as God had led them into the land and subdued it before them.

The only promise remaining to be fulfilled was the promise of a great blessing to come upon all nations. That was fulfilled many years later when Jesus came to die for all men's sins. Meanwhile, until that promise was fulfilled, God worked with the nation of Israel, trying to keep them faithful. This becomes the story of the rest of the Old Testament until the birth of Jesus.

Study Notes on Joshua and Ruth

Joshua 22

Joshua 22 - Tribes East of Jordan Sent Home and Build an Altar

22:1-5 — Joshua commended the eastern tribes for fulfilling their responsibilities.

During Moses' lifetime, Israel had captured the land east of Jordan. The tribes of Reuben, Gad, and half the tribe of Manasseh had been granted permission to settle this land for their inheritance. However, before they could return home to settle their own land, God had required them to go with the other tribes to help capture the land west of Jordan. Joshua had required these 2½ tribes to keep this agreement. See Numbers 32; Joshua 1:12-18.

At the present point in the account, Israel had captured the territory west of Jordan and had been given their designated inheritances. The 2½ tribes had fulfilled their agreement. Joshua here called these tribes to him and praised them for completing the task they had agreed to do. He plainly stated that they had obeyed God's command, so now they should return home to care for their own inheritance.

Before they left, however, Joshua admonished them to obey God's commands, hold fast to them, and serve God with all their heart and soul.

These tribes would face special challenges being east of the river. They would be somewhat remote from the rest of Israel. They would be closest in contact with other nations surrounding Israel on the east. This would create military difficulties and could create problems spiritually. They might be tempted to feel isolated from the worship of God and contact with surrounding nations might lead them to be tempted to participate in false worship. So Joshua gave them this special admonition to be faithful.

22:6-9 – Joshua blessed the 2½ tribes and sent them home.

Before sending them to their inheritance, Joshua pronounced a blessing on them. He said that they had gained many spoils in the victory over the nations of the land. They would return with livestock, silver, gold, bronze, iron, and much clothing. These should be divided with the people of their tribes.

So the soldiers departed to go to their inheritance.

22:10-14 – The 2½ tribes built an altar, so the other tribes assembled to go to war against them.

Having reached the river Jordan, the men of Reuben, Gad, and half of Manasseh built an altar. It was great and impressive. I am not clear which side of the river it occupied, east or west. The account says it was on the children of Israel's side, which sounds west.

This was reported to the tribes west of Jordan, and they became greatly concerned about it. We will see that they feared that the tribes east of Jordan intended to worship God separately apart from the tribes west of Jordan. So all Israel gathered together to go to war against the 2½ tribes.

Before attacking, however, they had the good sense to send a delegation to discuss the matter with the 2½ tribes. They sent Phinehas, son of Eleazar the high priest, and with him they sent a chief ruler from each of the 9½ tribes west of Jordan – a total of ten rulers.

22:15-20 – The 9½ tribes reminded the eastern tribes of past sins in the nation and so asked them why they had built an altar.

The delegation from the western tribes warned the eastern tribes not to change the pattern of worship that God had ordained. They warned that building the altar would be rebelling and turning away from God.

To illustrate their concern they referred to recent instances known to all the people in which Israelites had sinned against God. In the matter of Peor the people had worshipped idols and had committed fornication. As a result, God killed many in a plague (Numbers 25). Achan also had sinned by taking things that had been devoted to God in the fall of Jericho. He was slain (Joshua 7).

But beside their concern for the tribes east of Jordan, the other tribes were concerned that God would be angry with them for not opposing such a departure. They said if the 2½ tribes rebelled, then God would be angry the next day with the whole nation.

Study Notes on Joshua and Ruth

They evidently remembered the lesson learned from the case of Achan. One man sinned, but the whole nation could not prosper until they punished him. Likewise, they were implying that the nation would be responsible to punish the eastern tribes for their sin or God would hold the whole nation accountable.

They said that they would be willing to give the eastern tribes land where they could settle west of Jordan, if they would at least worship properly. This would be better than taking the inheritance they wanted east of Jordan, if this led them to worship improperly.

Note that they here state plainly their concern. By dwelling in a land so far from the tabernacle of the Lord, the eastern tribes might worship at a separate altar than the one the Lord had designated. They had built another altar, and Israel's concern was that the eastern tribes would not come to the altar at the tabernacle to offer their worship as God had required (Deuteronomy 12:5-14). So, they said for the eastern tribes to move in among the western tribes if necessary to avoid this sin. Note that the sin, which here concerned Israel, did later occur when the northern tribes of Israel separated from the southern tribes of Judah.

22:21-29 – The eastern tribes explained that they did not intend to use the altar for worship but to remind all the tribes that they were part of the nation of Israel.

The tribes from east of Jordan then responded and explained their purpose in building the altar. They said that they knew it would be wrong to use the altar to worship away from the altar God had designated for offering their various sacrifices. They said if they were to do such a thing as that, then the other tribes would be right in attacking them and God Himself ought to punish them.

But they said their real reason was in essence the very opposite. First, they affirmed several times that they had no intention to use the altar as a place to offer sacrifice of any kind. Instead, the altar was to serve as a reminder to future generations that the eastern tribes were part of Israel and they should be included in the worship of God at His designated place.

They feared that future generations might conclude that, since these tribes lived east of Jordan, they were not part of Israel's worship to God. People might want to exclude them from worshipping at the true altar. So they built this altar as a witness to remind future generations that they too were servants of God and should worship at the altar in Israel.

22:30-34 – *Israel accepted the explanation of the eastern tribes and returned home peaceably.*

Phinehas and the leaders of the western tribes were glad to hear this explanation from the eastern tribes. They rejoiced that the eastern tribes had not committed treachery against God. In so doing, they had avoided God's displeasure from coming on the nation.

They then returned to the western tribes and explained the purpose of the altar as intended by the eastern tribes. This brought joy to all the people of the western tribes, so they realized they did not need to go to war against their own people.

The Reubenites and Gadites then named the altar "Witness," because that was its purpose: a witness to all the tribes that the eastern tribes recognized the God of Israel as the true God.

Lessons to be learned from this event

1) We must worship God in the way He has commanded. Unauthorized worship is unacceptable, even if it is not specifically condemned in Scripture.

2) People in the congregation must be rebuked and opposed when they sin. If God's people do not rebuke the sin, even if we do not participate in it, God holds us accountable.

3) Before disciplining those who we think might be guilty of sin, we must communicate with them to be sure we understand what has been done and why. We may find that people have not done what we thought they did. John 7:24

4) If people are not guilty of sin, we should have unity and rejoice in the peace that results.

5) While the 2½ tribes may not have actually sinned here, better judgment would have shown them that what they were doing would be likely to appear sinful to others. The wiser course of action, that would have avoided the conflict, would have been to discuss their intent with the other tribes before actually building the altar.

Likewise, mature judgment in our service to God should lead us to anticipate problems that may result from our conduct and discuss these concerns with other people who may otherwise misunderstand.

Study Notes on Joshua and Ruth

Joshua 23

Joshua's final discourses
- Joshua 23,24

Joshua 23 - Joshua's Warning to the People

23:1-5 — When Joshua was old, he called Israel together and reminded them how God had given them the land and divided it among them.

These events happened a long time later after God had given Israel rest from wars with the surrounding nations, after Joshua was old. He later died at age 110 (24:29); however, Joshua had been said to be old as far back as 13:1. We are not told how long had passed since the land was conquered nor how long it was from the time of this message till Joshua died. However, at least some considerable time must have passed since Israel had divided the land till Joshua gave this parting message.

He called all Israel, along with their leaders, and rehearsed how he had led them into the land. He said that God had fought for them, so they had captured the land and had divided it among them from the Jordan to the Great Sea (Mediterranean). He promised that God would continue to expel the other nations from the land so that Israel could completely possess it for themselves alone (Ex. 23:30). Later in the message he attached conditions to this.

However, this is not to deny that the land had all been given to them. He clearly stated that it had been all given to them and he would repeat this again (21:43-45; 23:14). So the land was theirs. There was no doubt that they possessed it, but there were still people of other nations living in it in certain areas where Israel had not driven them out. And several tribes had yet to move in and take physical possession of their lands (see on Judges 1.)

23:6-10 – *Joshua warned them to keep God's law, be faithful to Him, and avoid the idolatry of the peoples of the land.*

Joshua's final admonition to Israel contains some of the same instructions that the book began with in reciting God's instructions to him when he began to lead the nation (1:5-9). He warned the people to have the courage to do all that God taught in Moses' law, not turning from it to the right or the left.

They were not to in any way compromise with the gods of the people remaining among them. They not only were not to bow in worship to those gods nor swear by them, they were not even to mention them. Instead, they were to hold fast and be faithful to the true God.

He reminded them that by God's power they had driven out all the nations from the land; no one had been able to withstand them successfully. God had promised that one of them could chase a thousand, because God was fighting for them as He had promised to do. This promise was being repeated from Deuteronomy 28:7 and Leviticus 26:8. The point is that by God's power they would be victorious, and their enemies could not defeat them.

23:11-13 – *Joshua warned that if they associated and intermarried with the nations of the land, God would not drive out those nations but would leave them as a snare to Israel.*

Whereas Joshua promised God would continue to drive out the inhabitants if Israel was faithful, he here warned that this promise was conditional. If they did not remain true in loving God but allowed themselves to grow attached to the people, God would not continue to drive out the people of the land.

If they clung to the people of the nations, associating with them and making permanent bonds with them such as intermarriage, these people would cause Israel to sin. They would be like a trap or scourge and thorns in their eyes. God would not continue to remove the people of other nations from the land. On the contrary, the Israelites themselves would be removed from the land.

Note the clearly conditional nature of the land promise. God had given them the land in fulfillment of His promise to the fathers. He was willing even to remove the remnant of the people of the nations from the land. But whether or not He did that and whether or not Israel would remain in the land would depend on their faithfulness in obedience to Him. Receiving the land was unconditional. Keeping it was conditional. See Leviticus 26:14-33; Deuteronomy 28:15-68.

The record of Israel's history after this point, of course, shows they were not faithful and were therefore eventually removed from the land as God promised here and elsewhere.

23:14-16 – Joshua reminded them again that God had kept all His promises to them, but if they disobeyed they would be removed from the land and punished.

Joshua then again affirmed that God had kept His promises to Israel. He had done everything He promised to do. Nothing had failed. Compare 21:44,45. As mentioned before, this absolutely disproves the claims of modern premillennialists. They claim the land promise was not completely fulfilled, so it must be fulfilled when Jesus returns. Joshua absolutely denies their claim. Israel received all God had promised.

For further information, see our articles on premillennialism at our Bible Instruction web site at www.gospelway.com/instruct/.

But then Joshua repeated the conditional nature of keeping the land. They had received it. But whether or not they kept it depended on their future obedience. As surely as God had blessed them in giving them the land, He would just as surely punish them in the future if they did not keep His covenant. His anger would burn against them and they would be destroyed from off the land if they worshipped and served idols.

Joshua 24

Joshua 24 - Joshua's Parting Speech and Death

24:1-4 – Joshua began summarizing Israel's history. God called Abraham to Canaan and gave him many descendants. Jacob went down into Egypt.

Joshua's time to die drew near. He sought to give a final admonition to the people before his death. So he called the people to him, along with all their officers and judges. They met at Shechem. Shechem was located the middle of Canaan between Mt. Gerizim and Mt. Ebal (see **map**). This was the area where Joshua had the people hear the blessings and the cursings from the law in 8:30-35.

Joshua spoke as a prophet for God and revealed to the people a message from God. He began by summarizing the history of God's dealings with Israel. This became a common approach for dealing with the nation (compare Acts 7).

He began with Terah, father of Abraham and Nahor. Terah had lived beyond the river (Euphrates) and there had served other gods. This implies that Abraham also served other gods, but perhaps not necessarily.

In any case, Abraham surely became a follower of the true God. God called him and he followed God's command to move into Canaan. There God gave to Abraham his son Isaac and to Isaac his sons Esau and Jacob. To Esau God gave the land of Seir or Edom, but Jacob and his descendants went down into Egypt where they became slaves.

24:5-8 – Through the leadership of Moses, God brought plagues on Egypt and led Israel out of bondage. He gave them the land east of the Jordan.

God then described how He had sent Moses and Aaron and brought plagues on Egypt, so as to compel them to let Israel leave. Then he brought Israel to the Red Sea, pursued by the Egyptians.

Study Notes on Joshua and Ruth

There the people cried to the Lord and He separated Israel from the Egyptians by darkness and eventually caused the Egyptians to drown in the sea.

Israel had seen God's great miracles in Egypt and at the Red Sea, yet they had sinned against God and been compelled to wander in the wilderness. Finally, God brought them to the land east of Jordan. The Amorites fought with them, but God gave Israel victory so they could possess the land.

All this history was clearly known to the Israelites, yet God reviewed it to remind them of His great blessings to them.

24:9-13 – Balak hired Balaam to curse Israel, but God refused to listen. Then God gave Israel victory over all the lands of Canaan.

God then described how Balak, king of Moab, had called Balaam to bring a curse upon Israel so Moab could defeat Israel. However, God did not heed Balaam's desires but instead made him pronounce blessings on Israel. So God delivered Israel from Balaam's intentions.

Then God brought Israel into the Promised Land itself, west of Jordan. There the people of Jericho and other people of the land fought against Israel, but God gave Israel the victory. He fought for Israel, even sending the hornet to demoralize their enemies before Israel physically attacked them. This is not mentioned directly elsewhere in Joshua, but it had been predicted in Exodus 23:27,28; Deuteronomy 7:20. Here Joshua confirmed that it had happened. So ultimately the victory was not achieved by the power of Israel's weapons but by God's power.

God then gave the land to Israel. They were enabled to live in cities they had not built and eat crops they had not planted. God richly blessed them by bringing them into the land and giving them the fruits of other people's labors. They had not done the work to build up the land, and in many ways they had not done the work to conquer it (God had). Though they were required to meet conditions that involved work and even hard work, yet they had not earned the blessings God gave. This is the essence of grace.

24:14,15 – Joshua challenged Israel to serve God rather than the idols. He stated his intent that he and his family would serve the true God.

Having described God's goodness and blessings to Israel, Joshua challenged them to fear the Lord and serve Him in sincerity and truth (compare John 4:23,24). They should put away all other gods and serve the Lord.

He identified the gods they should put away as: (1) The gods their fathers served on the other side of the river (verses 14,15). This appears to refer to the gods served by Terah and the family when they lived across the Euphrates before God called Abraham (as described also in verse 2). (2) The gods of Egypt that some served when they were there. (3) The gods of the Amorites who dwelt in and around Canaan. All these gods were false gods, had not blessed Israel, and should not be served. The people should serve the true God, the God of Abraham, who had brought them out of Egypt and into Canaan.

They ought to serve the true God, so Joshua challenged them to make up their minds to do so. If they would not serve God, then which of these other gods would they serve? This appears to contrast God to these false gods, to help Israel see that the other gods were surely a poor choice.

Finally, Joshua stated the choice he and his family had made. They would serve the true God. Of course, this was the choice he was urging all Israel to make.

Note that people do have the power to choose for themselves religiously. We are not robots having no power to choose for ourselves. Nor are we predestined by unconditional election, so God has made the choice for us and we can do nothing except follow the compulsion where His Spirit leads us, as Calvinism teaches. Rather, we are creatures with the power to choose for ourselves, because God has granted us that power. We may choose incorrectly, but God will allow us to make that choice. He will ultimately punish us for such a wrong choice, but He will grant us the freedom now to make the choice. See also Genesis 2:16,17; 3:1-7; 1 Corinthians 10:13; Hebrews 4:15; 11:25; 1 Kings 18:21; Psalm 119:30.

For further information about man's power to choose, see our articles about individual responsibility in salvation and about election (predestination) at our Bible Instruction web site at <u>www.gospelway.com/instruct/</u>.

However, as parents, we are responsible to make the best choice for ourselves and then teach it to our children. We cannot, of course, ultimately decide for them. When they are on their own, they will exercise their power to choose for themselves. But we can forbid all evil in our own homes, whether the evil of idolatrous worship or any other evil acts. And we can insist that those subject to us learn about the true God and be urged in every possible way to serve Him. This was the choice Joshua made for his family. See Proverbs 22:6; Ephesians 6:4; Titus 2:4; Genesis 18:19.

Study Notes on Joshua and Ruth

*24:16-18 – The people affirmed their desire to serve the
Lord, because He had delivered them from Egypt and
given them the land of Canaan.*

The people responded to Joshua's challenge, as he had hoped
they would, by committing themselves to serve the true God. They
sought to put far from them the service of other gods or the
forsaking of the true God.

They recognized the Lord as the God who had brought them
from slavery in Egypt, had done great miracles before them, and
had cared for them and met their needs as they had traveled
through the wilderness. Furthermore, God had driven out before
them the people of the land and had given the land to them. So they
ought to serve the Lord as the true God.

This is exactly what Joshua had taught them. It was the correct
response, and it was the response Joshua sought. The people
recognized God's blessings to them and their obligation to serve
Him, not other gods. We should do the same.

*24:19-24 – Joshua warned the people of the seriousness of
their commitment, but the people bore witness that
they would serve the Lord and put away other gods.*

When the people stated their commitment to serve the true
God, Joshua warned them of the seriousness of the commitment.
He went so far as to tell them they could not serve Him, because His
requirements were so high. He is a holy God, who requires holiness
of His people. He is a jealous God, who would not forgive their sins
and unfaithfulness. If they left Him to serve other Gods, He would
consume and destroy them, despite all the good He had done them
in the past.

Surely these statements are hyperbole – exaggeration for
purpose of making a point, like verses such as Luke 14:26ff. Surely
God is willing to forgive. The animal sacrifices they had then could
not effectively remove sin (Heb. 10:1-17), but they offered
forgiveness and actually obtained it provisionally until Jesus' death
gave the permanent forgiveness (Heb. 9:15).

God is a God of love who had done many wonderful things for
them and now has sent His Son as the perfect sacrifice for our sins.
So, He is a holy and jealous God, but He is also willing to forgive
and surely He wanted them to serve Him. So, Joshua must have
been making a point so they would realize their need to commit
themselves truly to His service.

Clearly the people did not believe serving God was impossible,
for they proceeded to affirm their determination to serve God
despite Joshua's statement. And Joshua himself surely did not

mean that serving God was impossible, for He then accepted their choice.

He reinforced their commitment by calling upon witnesses to ratify it, much like legal contracts today may require witnesses to verify the transaction. But in this case the witnesses were the people themselves. Joshua called on them to serve as witnesses that they really intended to make this commitment. Of course, the point of all this was to solemnly emphasize the seriousness of this decision, so they would realize they should not back out or violate it.

The people then persisted in the commitment. They agreed that they were witnesses to one another's commitment. They affirmed that the Lord would be their God and they would obey His voice. So Joshua called upon them to put away other gods.

24:25-28 – Joshua set up a stone as a witness to the covenant the people had made to serve God.

This agreement made by the people is here called a covenant or solemn agreement. In reality it was just a renewal of the covenant the people had made with God when the law had been given at Mt. Sinai (Ex. 24:1-8). But it is here called a covenant, a statute, and an ordinance.

Joshua recorded it in the Book of the Law of God. This is the term used for the Book Moses had written (see Deut. 31:24-26 and compare Ex. 24:1-8 above). This shows that Joshua continued to write by inspiration in that Book.

Joshua then took a large stone and set it by an oak near the sanctuary. He said the stone would serve as a witness to the people's covenant, because it had heard what the Lord had spoken. Of course, it had not literally heard, but it had been there and now served the purpose of a permanent witness that the people had committed themselves to serve God. If they thought to deny Him, the stone would testify of their covenant.

Joshua then let the people return to their homes.

Note again how stones were used as witnesses to confirm commitments. See notes on chapter 4 for a similar example and notes there about other examples. This helps us see why God chose to write the 10 Commands on tables of stone. This was the formal way in that day of confirming a covenant, at least among Israel.

Note also that this verse implies that the sanctuary of the Lord was at this time at Shechem, whereas earlier (and again later) it was at Shiloh (see on 18:1-10, etc.). Note on the map that Shiloh and Shechem were quite close to one another. Perhaps the covenant was made at Shechem, but the stone was then moved the short distance to Shiloh and set up by the sanctuary there.

Study Notes on Joshua and Ruth

24:29-31 – Joshua died at age 110 and was buried in his inheritance. The people served the Lord all his days and the days of the other leaders who outlived him.

After this Joshua died at the age of 110 years old. He was buried at the edge (border) of his inheritance at Timnath Serah in Ephraim on the north side of Mt. Gaash. This inheritance had been given him as recorded in 19:50.

Israel had served the Lord all the days of Joshua and of the leaders (elders) who outlived him but had been alive to see all that the Lord had done for Israel in bringing them into the land. This shows that the generation who made the covenant was willing to keep it. In doing so, they were at least better than the previous generation.

The implication is that the people did not remain faithful in following generations. This is borne out in the book of Judges.

Here again we read the death of a great man of God. Death is the common lot of all mankind, no matter how good. Yet it is sad when we read of it. Joshua had done great work for God and for the people. He had led them into the land, defeated the enemies, and led them in faithfulness throughout his lifetime. In a sense even Moses had not accomplished that.

24:32,33 – Joseph's bones were buried in Shechem. Also the high priest Eleazar died and was buried.

Other interesting notes about great men of God are recorded to close the book.

Joseph had made the people of Israel swear that they would take his bones with them when they left Egypt to go back to Canaan (see Gen. 50:25). Hebrews 11:22 speaks of this as an act of faith, because it showed that Joseph was convinced the people would really return to receive the land as God had promised. Exodus 13:19 had recorded that the people did take his bones with them when they left.

Here we are told that his bones were not only brought into Canaan but were buried in Shechem in a plot of ground that had been bought by Jacob from the father of Shechem as recorded in Genesis 33:19. This area was included in the territory that Joseph's son Ephraim had inherited.

Finally, we are told of the death of Eleazar the high priest. Just as Joshua had succeeded Moses, so Eleazar had succeeded his father Aaron as high priest. See Numbers 20:22-29. He had served during Joshua's period as leader. Here we are told also of his death. He was buried in a plot of land belonging to his son Phinehas also in the mountains of Ephraim.

Ruth Chapter 1

Introduction

Author

The inspired author of the book cannot be determined for certain. Horne states, "...the most probable, and indeed generally received opinion, is that of the Jews, who state it to have been written by the prophet Samuel."

Theme

The character and devotion of Ruth, great grandmother of David

Main Characters

Ruth, Naomi, Boaz

Time period

These events occurred during the period when judges ruled (1:1). We are not given a more specific time frame than this. Apparently, we do not need to have more specific information, else God would have given it.

For me personally, the book of Judges is one of the most depressing books of the Bible, as the people of Israel again and again disobeyed God's law and had to be punished. Yet interestingly, the book of Ruth occurred during the period of the Judges, yet it is one of the most beautiful and uplifting stories of the Bible.

(For those who wish to pursue the question of exactly when this story occurred during the period of the Judges, you may wish to read Bob and Sandra Waldron's introduction to the book. However, in my view the evidence is not conclusive.)

Study Notes on Joshua and Ruth

Chapter 1 - Naomi and Ruth Return to Israel from Moab.

1:1,2 – In the days of the judges, Elimelech moved his wife Naomi and their two sons from Bethlehem of Judea to Moab because of a famine.

The story begins by introducing us to the family of Naomi. Naomi lived with her husband and her two sons in Bethlehem of Judah in the days of the judges (see **map**). Naomi's husband was named Elimelech, and her two sons were named Mahlon and Chilion. Bethlehem is also called Ephrath (Genesis 35:19; 48:7), so Elimelech is here called an Ephrathite. (Compare Micah 5:2; Ruth 4:11; 1 Samuel 17:12.)

Because there was a famine in the land, the family moved to live in the country of Moab. There they remained for a number of years. The Moabites lived east of the Dead Sea, especially between the Arnon and Zered rivers (see **map**).

1:3,4 – In Moab Elimelech died, and his sons married Moabite women, Ruth and Orpah.

While the family lived in Moab, Naomi's husband died leaving just her and her two sons. Next we are told that the two sons married women of Moab. Mahlon married a woman named Ruth (4:10), and Chilion married a woman named Orpah. We are then told that they lived there for 10 years.

Why did these Jews marry non-Jews in light of the passages forbidding intermarriage to people of other nations under the law?

God had repeatedly warned the people of Israel not to marry people of the lands where God would lead them. See Exodus 34:10-16; Deut. 7:1-5; Josh. 23:12,13; Nehemiah 9:30; 13:23-27; Ezra 9 & 10; etc. Note in particular that Ezra and Nehemiah criticized Jewish men of their day specifically for marrying women of Moab (Ezra 9:1,2; Nehemiah 13:23).

The original instruction as given by God (Exodus 34:10-16; Deuteronomy 7:1-5), however, does not mention Moabites. And it specifically states that the law applied to Israelites when God brought them into the land of their possession (Canaan). In Numbers 25:1,2 it was Moabite women who seduced the men of Israel to commit idolatry even before they entered Canaan. In any case it is specifically clear from those contexts that the problem of such intermarriage was that these foreigners would worship other gods and would lead the people of Israel away from serving the true God.

Possible explanation are:

(1) Perhaps Mahlon and Chilion sinned here. Nothing in the context requires that they be viewed as upright or godly men. Even if they were godly in general, they could have erred here. Naomi appears to be godly, at least by the time she leaves Moab, but we are told nothing about the godliness of her husband or sons. (It is possible from the language that Naomi's sons married Moabite women after their father had died.) Still, this leaves us with no explanation for why Boaz married Ruth, since he was apparently a godly man and knew she was a Moabite.

Matthew Henry implies many commentators believe the sons did sin here. He even criticizes Elimelech for taking his family to live among the idolatrous Moabite influence. Other Israelites apparently stayed in Canaan despite the famine. Surely it was unwise to move to live among idol worshipers, and this act occasioned the sons' marriage to Moabite women. As when Lot moved his family to live among the wicked people of Sodom, great tragedies followed in his family when Elimelech chose to move to Moab. Naomi clearly came to believe that her suffering and affliction were judgments or chastisements brought on her by God – see verses 13,20,21.

(2) Perhaps the Old Testament prohibited intermarriage, not with people of all other nations, but only with people of the nations that had dwelt in Canaan. Those nations were known to be excessively idolatrous. God cast them out of the land and gave it to Israel because the iniquity of those nations was "full." They surrounded Israel and so would be a continual temptation to them.

These reasons did not apply to other nations, and the prohibition is nowhere stated regarding them. In particular, such reasons might not apply to Moabites, since they were distantly related to Israelites. However, this does not explain why Ezra and Nehemiah rebuked men of Israel for marrying Moabite women.

(3) One conclusion that appears clear is that the prohibition applied only to women who were idolatrous, not to women who had converted to the true God and His true law (a "proselyte"). In particular, by the time Boaz married Ruth, she had proved beyond doubt to all the people who knew her that she served the true God and was known for her godliness. (Note that Orpah, on the other hand, is later said to have gone back to the god of her people – 1:15.)

Study Notes on Joshua and Ruth

1:5-7 — After her sons had died, Naomi determined to return to Judah, accompanied by her two daughters-in-law.

After this period of time had passed, Naomi's sons also died, so that she was left without husband or sons. Then she determined that she would return to the country of Judah, because she had heard by this time that the famine had been relieved and the people now had food. So she arose with her daughters-in-law to leave the country of Moab.

1:8,9 — Naomi then urged her daughters-in-law to return to their parents' homes.

Naomi told her daughters-in-law that they had dealt kindly with her, especially in being willing to return with her to Judah. However, she believed that it was better for them to return to the families of their parents. She asked a blessing from the Lord upon them that He would deal kindly with them even as they had dealt kindly with her and with her dead family members. She expressed the hope that the Lord would grant each of them rest in the house of her husband. This would appear to imply that she hoped that they would remarry.

So the ladies kissed one another and wept. This shows that they had become quite close to one another in the period of time that they had lived together as a family. Naomi was sending them back, not because she did not care for them, but because she believed it would be best for them. Families should seek to develop the kind of closeness with one another that they enjoy being together, but parting becomes a source of grief.

The Waldrons point out that, when a woman married, she became part of her husband's family. Even if the husband died, she was still expected to continue as part of that family, and it would be their responsibility to care for her. But in this case, Naomi had no one to care for her, let alone to care for her daughters-in-law. So, if the daughters would return to the homes of their parents, they would have someone to take care of them, and may eventually be able to remarry. While laws and customs today may differ from those days, nevertheless the New Testament also encourages young widows to remarry – 1 Timothy 5:14.

1:10-13 — When the daughters-in-law wanted to stay with Naomi, she explained that she had no sons for them to marry.

At first, both Ruth and Orpah expressed the determination to stay with Naomi and return with her to her people. This shows the close relationship that Naomi had with her daughters-in-law. We learn more about their strong devotion to one another as the story proceeds.

This is admirable. Families should seek to develop this kind of love and unity for one another, even with those who marry into the family. Do we seek to show love and kindness towards our in-laws as is demonstrated in this story?

But Naomi explained to them that she had no sons for them to marry. In those days, as we will see as the story progresses, if a woman became a widow but had no children to inherit her husband's property, it would become the responsibility of one of her husband's brothers (or other relatives) to marry her and raise up children to inherit the dead husband's property. But Naomi is explaining that she had no sons for these young ladies to marry.

Obviously, both of Naomi's sons had died and she had no other sons. She asked the rhetorical question of whether or not she had sons in her womb to grow up that the girls might marry them. Of course, the answer is that she had no sons. And she explained she was too old now to have a husband and bear other sons in the future. And besides, if she did have other sons, the girls would have to wait for them to grow up before they could marry. So, Naomi expressed her great grief at the difficulties of their circumstances, but she believed it was best for the girls to return to their parents' homes.

Note that here is one of the places where Naomi clearly stated that she believed she was suffering because of the hand of the Lord. See also verses 20,21. She could, of course, have been mistaken about this even as Job was. See Job 1:21; 2:10; and many other places in the book of Job. However, in the case of Job we are clearly told that he was upright and was not suffering because of his sins. No such statements are made regarding Naomi or her family.

The Bible shows that God often does allow suffering in the lives of those who need to be chastised – see Hebrews 12:5-11. So, while it is possible that Naomi is mistaken here, it is also possible that she is correct. This would harmonize with the fact that the sons may have sinned in marrying Moabite women, and perhaps even that her husband may have sinned or shown a lack of wisdom in even moving to Moab.

1:14,15 – Orpah then chose to return to her own family, so Naomi urged Ruth to do likewise.

After this urging from Naomi, the women wept again, but then Orpah did as Naomi had suggested and returned to her own people. Ruth, however, determined to remain with Naomi. So Naomi once

Study Notes on Joshua and Ruth

again urged Ruth to return to her own family even as Orpah had done.

Why would Naomi urge her daughters-in-law to return to their families knowing that they were idol worshipers?

I find it strange that the passage says that Orpah had returned, not only to her family, but also to her gods. And perhaps even more strange, Naomi appears to be encouraging Ruth to do the same thing. Why would Naomi urge the girls to go back to their families, if she knew the result was that they would go back to the worship of false gods?

Consider some possibilities:

1. Could it be that these years had been such a traumatic time for Naomi, because of the famine and the deaths of her husband and sons, that she was so distraught she was not thinking clearly? In her time of great grief, could it be that she herself was wavering in faith?

2. A better explanation is that Naomi was simply urging the girls to count the cost of going with her. Maybe she did not really want them to return home, but she wanted them to make sure that they understood the consequences of going with her. No doubt she would very much have appreciated their companionship had they gone with her. So in that sense it is clear that she would rather they had not returned to their Moabite families.

But going with Naomi to Israel would have been far harder on these girls than they may well have realized. In her wisdom, Naomi would have understood the consequences better than the girls. Perhaps she wanted to make sure that they were not simply making a decision under the emotion of the circumstances but might change their minds after they had been in Israel for a while. Once they faced the difficulties in Israel, the emotional ties they felt for her at the moment may not have been sufficient to sustain them. They would have needed a greater commitment.

She had no prospects for their physical and material support. If she had sons to marry them, those sons of course would have supported their wives. But being an aged widow, how could she have supported them? Had they returned to Moab, their parental families could have cared for them until they found husbands to marry. They needed to realize the difficulties if they stayed with her.

Furthermore, they were moving into a land that was completely foreign to them. They did not know the nature of the people. But above all, they would not have understood the spiritual consequences of living in Israel. The Israelites were a nation unlike any other. Finding husbands among the Israelites may well have been impossible due to the prohibitions against marrying foreign women. The Israelites did not view their God as simply a god but as the only true God. Unless the girls converted to faith in the true God, they would be aliens living in Israel, spiritually as well as in nationality.

Naomi understood the consequences of all this, but the girls probably did not. Perhaps she was just testing them to see how strong their commitment was. Unless they demonstrated truly strong commitment, they would soon be miserable in Israel and might decide to return to Moab anyway. Orpah did not demonstrate this commitment, so she returned home. Ruth, however, clearly demonstrated that she did have this commitment, so Naomi gladly welcomed her to go with her – see verse 16.

The Bible contains a number of other examples in which people are urged to count the cost before making commitments that they might later regret.

Luke 14:26-33; Matthew 8:19,20; 19:21,22 – Jesus made statements that sound like He is discouraging people from becoming His disciples. But in reality, He is simply challenging them to count the cost of being His disciples. People need to consider before they become followers of Jesus the difficulties that will be involved, rather than beginning His service and having second thoughts later.

Joshua 24:16-22 – When the people of Israel claimed they would serve the Lord, Joshua warned them that God is a jealous God. He may appear to be discouraging them from following God, but obviously was simply trying to get them to recognize the seriousness of the commitment so they did not change their minds later.

When a couple is considering getting married, in a similar way they need to be urged to think seriously about the commitment that they are making. The time to consider the consequences of a serious commitment is before we enter into it, rather than professing the commitment and then changing our minds.

1:16-18 – Ruth then beautifully expressed her devotion to Naomi and to the true God.

In her beautiful and poetic response, Ruth urged Naomi not to ask her to leave or to go back.

She insisted that she would go wherever Naomi would go and lodge wherever Naomi would lodge. She was going to a country where she had never been before, far from her own family and her own homeland. Yet her commitment was that she would gladly go.

She was willing to accept Naomi's people as her own people. Even though they were a completely different nationality from her

Study Notes on Joshua and Ruth

own – a nationality that many of her own people hated – she was willing to devote herself to learning to live among them.

And even most important, she had come to believe in the true God and was determined to accept God as her own God. This devotion explained her determination to remain with Naomi. It is especially essential to the subsequent story to understand that Ruth had come to a true faith in the true God.

She affirmed that she would continue with Naomi until death and even be buried where Naomi would be buried. She was determined that nothing would tempt her to go back to her own family and homeland. She would stay with Naomi until death.

In what amounts to a promise before God, she affirms that nothing but death would part her from Naomi. So on hearing this response, Naomi realized that Ruth was determined to go with her, so she ceased asking her to leave.

This speech is often quoted in wedding ceremonies as a beautiful expression of the devotion of a husband and wife. Obviously, it was spoken originally as the devotion of a daughter-in-law to her mother-in-law. Nevertheless, it does express the beauty of strong family ties, and as such expresses very well the devotion of a husband and wife. In many ways this speech also describes the commitment that a Christian should have in following Jesus Christ. In fact, our devotion to Him should be even stronger to the point that not even death would separate us from Him.

1:19-22 – Naomi and Ruth were greeted with excitement when they arrived at Bethlehem. But Naomi expressed her great grief for her suffering.

Having returned from Moab to Israel, the ladies arrived at Naomi's hometown of Bethlehem. Naomi's family had been gone for at least ten years. She had faced many hardships. No doubt she had changed in many ways, including appearance. But the people she had known in years past recognized her and greeted her with excitement.

They asked if she was Naomi, perhaps in wonder at the changes in her. In any case, she responded asking them to call her, not Naomi, but Mara. Naomi means "pleasant," but Mara means "bitter" (see NKJV footnotes).

She explained that God had dealt bitterly with her. She had left home full with many blessings, but she had returned empty, having lost all the family she had when she left. So she thought a better name for her would be "bitter," because God had chosen to afflict her. She doubtless did not really intend to change her name, since she is called "Naomi" through the rest of the story. But she was simply expressing her deep grief.

Here is another place in which Naomi expressed her conviction that God had dealt bitterly with her, afflicted her, and testified against her. This is how she viewed her circumstances. See notes on verse 13. It is possible that her problems were not really a chastisement by God, but it is apparent that she believed they were. If this is how God has treated us, we need to humbly submit to His chastisement even as Naomi did here.

So the women returned and dwelt in Bethlehem at the beginning of barley harvest (late March or early April). The harvest becomes important as the story proceeds.

Study Notes on Joshua and Ruth

Ruth Chapter 2

Chapter 2 - Ruth Gleans in the Field of Boaz.

2:1 – Introduction to Boaz: a wealthy relative of Naomi's husband

Next the account introduces us to the other major character in the story. His name was Boaz, and we are told that he was a relative of Naomi's husband. This relationship becomes of great significance as the story proceeds. We are also told that he was a man of great wealth. At this point we are simply introduced to him.

2:2,3 – Ruth went to glean in fields belonging to Boaz.

Ruth and Naomi obviously were poor at this point in the story. Naomi's family had left Israel in the first place because of the famine. Then in Moab all the males in the family had died. This meant that there were no men to provide income for the family. In God's plan for the family, the men are intended to be the primary workers to provide family income, while the women care for the home. But here the men had died, so the women were left to find some means of income for themselves.

Ruth suggested that she go into the fields and glean the grain in whatever field she might find where people would allow her to glean. Naomi agreed for her to go. So, Ruth went and gleaned in the field after the reapers.

To understand the story, it is helpful to understand the concept of gleaning, especially as taught under the Old Testament law. The law required that, when people would harvest their crops from their fields, any grain that fell to the ground must be left. This was a way of providing for the poor, widows, orphans, and strangers – three of these categories would apply to Ruth. It was understood that those who lacked for themselves would be free to go into the fields and gather whatever grain had fallen to the ground. This was called gleaning. This law applied to grain in the fields or to grapes in a vineyard or olive trees, etc. See Leviticus 19:9,10; 23:22; Deuteronomy 24:19-22.

Notice what we learn about Ruth here. First, she was standing by her commitment to remain with Naomi and Naomi's people. Gleaning was hard work, suited only to those who were poor. Yet Ruth did not seek to return to Moab or expect other people to provide for her. She was willing to do the work needed to provide for both herself and for Naomi.

Further, we see that Ruth was industrious and willing to humble herself to do a job suitable only to those who were poor. She did not lie around in bed or complain about her lot. She did not think the job was beneath her dignity, even though most likely it was a job she had never done before. She was energetic and determined to do what needed to be done.

As Ruth went to glean, apparently by chance she happened to glean in the field belonging to Boaz, the relative of Naomi's family. Now of course we will see that this was not really so much by chance. The providence of God was at work in the story. But here we begin to see the connection between Boaz and the well-being of Naomi and Ruth.

2:4-7 – Boaz became aware of Ruth, who was gleaning in his field and was from Moab but was the daughter-in-law of Naomi.

Remember that Boaz was a wealthy man. He lived in Bethlehem and doubtless had many possessions. Included were fields where the workers at this time were gathering in the harvest. So Boaz went to visit the laborers and see how the work went. Apparently in those days it was common for people who owned farm fields to live in a village or city, but their fields would lie surrounding the city. So the owners from time to time would go out to visit the workers in the field as Boaz did in this case.

Boaz greeted his reapers with kindness and even with spiritual concern. He asked for the Lord to be with them, and they responded by asking the Lord to bless him. What a blessing it is for laborers to have an employer who cares about them, and for employers and employees both to respect the will of God regarding work and regarding the treatment of one another. We begin to see that Boaz was not only a wealthy man but also a godly man.

Further, he was diligent and a hard worker. Many rich people would leave it up to servants to supervise the work of laborers, but Boaz was personally involved in meeting, supervising, and seeing firsthand what work was being done by his laborers.

Study Notes on Joshua and Ruth

As he observed the harvest, Boaz of course noticed Ruth working in the fields, so he asked the servant in charge of the reapers about her. The servant explained that she was the Moabite woman who came back with Naomi, who had returned from Moab. She had asked to glean after the reapers, and she had worked diligently throughout the day taking only a short rest in the house.

Note that we learn here that Ruth was still a young woman. It was not clear to me from chapter 1 exactly how long Ruth had been married before her husband died. But in any case she was young enough when she married that she was still a young woman at this point in the story.

Now Boaz was a relative of Naomi's husband and no doubt knew something about Naomi and her fortunes. Probably he even knew that she had gone to Moab and had returned. In any case, at this point he had been introduced to Ruth to whom he was related by marriage.

2:8,9 – Boaz urged Ruth to continue gleaning only in his fields. He had arranged for her to be protected and her needs provided.

Having learned who Ruth was, Boaz treated her with kindness. He urged her to not glean in any other fields except his. Evidently he believed he had enough of a harvest that she could provide her needs completely by working in his own fields. But he was also interested in protecting and providing for her.

So, he urged her to stay close to his female servants who were working in the fields. She should observe which field they would reap and she could follow. He assured her that his instructions to his menservants would protect her, so that they would not molest her in any way. And when she became thirsty she could even go and drink from the water vessels that had been provided for the workers.

Ruth was both a foreigner and a stranger to these people. Cruel people sometimes act unkindly toward people such as Ruth. They may shun or ridicule or make fun. Young men might make improper advances. By giving proper instructions to his servants and to Ruth, Boaz made sure that his workers would treat her properly and that she would stay where she was safe.

At the same time, Boaz did not discourage Ruth from doing her work. Poor people need to learn to do what they can to provide for themselves, and others should encourage them to do so. We may make provision to enable the poor to work for their necessities, but we should expect them to do what they can. We do no favor to those who are poor if we do for them what they can do for themselves. To provide for those who can provide for themselves, without expecting them to work, teaches them bad habits and insults their dignity. Those who will not work should not eat – 2 Thessalonians 3:10.

All this was unusual kindness to a gleaner. Boaz probably did this to some extent from the kindness of his nature, but also because of the things he had learned about Ruth (see verses 10-12).

2:10-13 – Boaz explained that he showed kindness and favor to Ruth because he had learned of her upright conduct.

When Ruth heard the kind words that Boaz had spoken to her, she bowed down before him to the ground. She asked him why he was being so good to her, that he had shown such favor and taken such notice of her, especially since she was a foreigner. At this point she knew nothing about him or his relationship to her. But she did know that she was from another country, so such kindness was surprising to her.

But Boaz responded that he did know about her. He said he had received a full report about how she had been so good to her mother-in-law since the death of her husband. Furthermore, he knew how she had left the land of her birth as well as her parents in order to come and live among a strange people. She had done all this by choice, since she could have gone back to her people like Orpah did, where she would have been provided for without such sacrifices. He called for the blessing of God to be upon her to repay her and give her a full reward for the work that she had done, since she had sought refuge under the protection of the God of Israel.

Note again that the response shows that Boaz himself was a devout religious man. It also implies that he was aware of Ruth's spiritual devotion to God. If she had sought refuge under the wings of the God of Israel, this would imply that she believed in the true God. She was no longer seeking to serve and seek the blessings of other gods.

Ruth responded that she sought favor in the sight of Boaz because of the kindly words that he had spoken to her. She realized she was not one of his maidservants, and yet he had treated her kindly as though she was.

Boaz had not explained to Ruth what his relationship to her was. He had only explained that he knew about her godly character and her good treatment of her mother-in-law. But surely if he knew all this about Ruth and Naomi, then he also knew that he was a near kinsman to Naomi and therefore to Ruth. He was aware of the relationship and of the consequences according to the law in ways about which Ruth would not have been aware.

Study Notes on Joshua and Ruth

And note some lessons we can learn regarding the choice of a marriage companion. Today people often emphasize physical matters in their choice: beauty, wealth, status, etc. Boaz said nothing about Ruth's appearance at any point (not that such is bad or wrong – she did later try to look nice to please him). She had no wealth. But what he emphasized throughout was her character and godliness. See Proverbs 31.

2:14-16 – Boaz encouraged Ruth to eat with his reapers, and told the reapers to make sure grain fell for Ruth to glean.

As the day continued, Boaz continued to make provisions for Ruth in ways of special kindness. When the mealtime came, he called upon her to come and eat with the reapers. She could eat of the bread and dip her bread in the vinegar. He passed parched grain to her to eat so that she was completely satisfied with her meal. She even kept some back which, we will see, she took home to Naomi. We may not think that dipping bread in vinegar would be tasty, but at least one commentator suggested that such a procedure is helpful for those who are exerting themselves in hard labor.

When the meal was completed and Ruth rose up again to glean, Boaz went further and instructed his young menservants to allow her to glean even among the sheaves. They were not to rebuke her for approaching so close to the grain. In fact, he instructed them to deliberately allow grain to fall from the bundles and leave it so that she could pick it up.

All of this went far beyond the normal treatment of those who would glean in a field. It would be one thing for grain that fell accidentally to be left there for the poor to glean. But it was another thing to allow them to glean even among the sheaves of grain as they were being harvested. This was not required by the law, let alone was it required that the workers would deliberately allow grain to fall. Obviously, all this was an expression of the kindness of Boaz toward Ruth.

Notice that truly good people show acts of kindness even when those to whom they are being kind do not necessarily know about the kindnesses. Far too often people want to do good only if they are going to be acknowledged and praised by others. Some of the greatest kindnesses are those that are unknown to those who benefit.

2:17,18 – At the end of the day Ruth returned home to Naomi and shared the results of her day's work.

So Ruth continued working in the field all day. At the end of the day she beat out the grain that she had gleaned, so it amounted to about an ephah of barley. The Waldrons say that an ephah amounts to about 20 to 25 pounds. That would be a significant amount of grain to glean in one day, and this was after she had removed the husks.

So Ruth returned home to Naomi and showed her the results of her day's work. She also gave Naomi the food that she had left over after she had finished her own meal. Please notice, exactly as Boaz had said, that Ruth was very kind and generous with her mother-in-law. Ruth had worked hard all day long, yet she was willing to completely share the fruits of her labors with Naomi.

2:19,20 – At Naomi's request, Ruth told her that she had worked in the field of Boaz. Naomi informed Ruth that he was a near relative.

Naomi was obviously impressed by the generous amount of grain that Ruth had been able to glean. So she asked where Ruth had gleaned, and even pronounced a blessing on the one who had taken notice of her. She apparently realized that such a generous amount of grain could only have come if someone had been quite nice to Ruth. So Ruth informed Naomi that she had worked in the field of a man named Boaz.

As we have mentioned, Ruth would not have known about their relationship to Boaz. But Naomi knew. She explained to Ruth that Boaz was a relation of theirs, even a close relative. Then she pronounced a blessing on the Lord because He had not forsaken them, either the living or the dead, but had shown them kindness. The living would refer to Naomi and Ruth who were still surviving, whereas the dead would refer to her husband and Ruth's husband, because they now had a relative who was being generous to their family. But the significance of the near kinsman also would relate to the inheritance of the dead men in the family.

2:21,22 – Ruth explained that Boaz wanted her to continue gleaning in his fields. Naomi heartily approved.

Ruth then continued to explain that, in addition to what she had already told Naomi, Boaz had also told Ruth to stay close to his workers throughout the rest of the harvest. This meant that Ruth would have a means to continue to provide for herself and Naomi.

Study Notes on Joshua and Ruth

They had not been blessed for just one day, but had hope for continued blessings throughout the rest of the harvest.

Naomi agreed that this was good, so she urged Ruth to continue to work only in the fields of Boaz with his maidservants. People should not see her in any other field. It is not clear at this point how much Ruth would understand about the role of a near kinsman, but obviously Naomi was beginning to understand where this might lead. The subsequent story will explain it.

Note how the story repeatedly states that Ruth should stay with the young women who worked in Boaz' fields (2:8,22,23; 3:2). (Boaz indicated that they followed the young men who worked the fields, but the young women evidently worked together in a group.) Modern society would do well to learn from this example. The passage clearly shows here, as elsewhere in Scripture, that the ideal situation for women is to marry and be workers at home, supported by their husbands. However, as in the case of Ruth, sometimes this is not possible, and some women may simply choose not to marry. Such women may need to find jobs outside the home. But far too often in the modern workplace, married women work alongside men other than their husbands. The result is far too often the establishment of relationships that lead to immorality. The arrangement that Naomi urged would help avoid such problems.

2:23 – Ruth continued to work in the fields of Boaz throughout the barley and the wheat harvest.

Apparently, all that has been discussed in this chapter up to this point happened in Ruth's first day working in the fields of Boaz. The story simply summarizes the rest of the harvest by saying that she did work in the fields of Boaz among his young women, not just for the rest of the barley harvest, but also for the rest of the wheat harvest. Meanwhile she continued to live with Naomi, no doubt sharing with her the fruits of her gleaning.

This is a brief summary. However, we can properly read between the lines that this period of time would have continued for several weeks. In the meantime no doubt Boaz would continue to observe Ruth and her work. Probably he continued to do some investigation in regard to the background of his relationship to Naomi's family. In any case, as the story proceeds it becomes clear that he knows a good bit about Ruth and about his responsibilities as a near kinsman.

Ruth Chapter 3

Chapter 3 - Ruth Requests Boaz to Fulfill the Role of a Near Kinsman.

3:1,2 – Naomi informed Ruth that Boaz is a near kinsman and she wanted to seek future security for Ruth.

As the harvest began drawing to a close, Naomi informed Ruth that she was determined to seek security for Ruth. She knew a way to provide for Ruth's well-being, which would of course also provide for Naomi. This depended upon Boaz. Naomi informed Ruth that Boaz was a relative – that is, a near kinsman. Ruth may not have understood the significance of this, but both Boaz and Naomi would have understood.

The role of the near kinsman

In order to understand the events of this chapter, one must have some concept of the role under the Old Testament of a near kinsman. In this case, two things were involved. First was the right to redeem property that had been sold by a relative. And second was the responsibility to raise up seed to a dead relative who had no children to inherit. These concepts are unfamiliar to us in our society, so we need to understand them to understand the story.

It must be remembered that ancestry was very important among the Jews, especially in order to inherit land in the promised land of Canaan. It was very important to families to make sure that their possession in Canaan remained in the family.

1) Raising up an heir to a brother who died childless – If a man died without a child, his property would pass out of the family. To avoid this, the law had provision as explained especially in Deuteronomy 25:5-10 (see also Genesis 38:8).

The law said that, in this case, the brother of the dead man should take the dead man's widow as his wife. Then the firstborn son that she would bear would inherit in the name of the dead brother, so that his name would not be blotted out of Israel.

Study Notes on Joshua and Ruth

This is sometimes called "Levirate marriage." The law provided that, if the man did not want to perform this duty, he may refuse, but he was subject to being humiliated before the elders of the city.

2) The law also provided that, if a man's property passed out of his possession – such as by being sold in time of financial distress – his relative could redeem the property to keep it in the family and especially in the tribe. See Numbers 36:9; 27:9-11; Leviticus 25:8-55, especially verses 23-34.

In the present story, Ruth's husband had died without child. Apparently, because of the famine and the death of Naomi's husband and Ruth's husband, their family property was also in danger of passing out of the family possession.

As a near kinsman, Boaz could redeem the property and could marry Ruth in order to raise up seed to Ruth's husband. However, we will see that there was another relative even closer than Boaz, which complicated the plans.

This was the time of the winnowing of the barley harvest at the threshing floor. So Naomi was sure that Boaz would be there.

3:3,4 – Ruth was to go to Boaz at the threshing floor when he laid down for the night, and she was to lie down at his feet.

Naomi instructed Ruth to wash herself and anoint herself and put on her best garment. No doubt this was to make her attractive. Then she was to go to the threshing floor and wait until Boaz had finished his meal and had lain down for the night. She was go to the place where he lay down, uncover his feet, and lie down at his feet. Naomi said that he would understand the significance of this and would instruct Ruth further.

3:5-7 – Ruth agreed and did as was instructed.

As Naomi had instructed, Ruth agreed and went to the threshing floor. After Boaz had finished his meal, he went to lie down at the end of the heap of grain. Ruth watched where he lay down, and she approached softly, uncovered his feet, and lay down.

The passage says that after Boaz had eaten and drunk, his heart was cheerful. This does not say that he was intoxicated. "Had drunk" is simply the past perfect form of drink. He had eaten and he had drunk. Nothing in the context states or implies that he had drunk anything intoxicating. His heart was merry or cheerful; but people are often happy after they have had a good meal, especially at a time of harvest when people naturally rejoice at the bringing in of the crop.

3:8,9 – When Boaz awoke during the night, Ruth asked him to do the role of a close relative.

Boaz did not realize that Ruth was lying at his feet until he awoke at midnight. As he turned over, he realized a woman was lying at his feet, so he asked who it was. Ruth identified herself and asked Boaz to fulfill the role of a close relative and take his maidservant under his wing. Knowing the law regarding the role of a near kinsman, Boaz would have understood exactly what Ruth was asking for.

Did Ruth here act in an immoral manner?

Some skeptics have argued that Ruth here attempted to seduce Boaz to an immoral sexual relationship. Others have tried to justify Ruth's conduct on the grounds that she and Boaz had the right to a sexual relationship because of the law of the near kinsman.

However, I see no reason to conclude that there was any attempt to seduce Boaz to a sexual relationship in what Ruth did. The law of the near kinsman said that he was to **marry** the widow of the dead relative. (Deuteronomy 25:5 says he should take her as "wife" – NKJV, ASV, KJV, NASB, ESV, "marry her" – NIV.) I see no reason to conclude that the near kinsman and the widow would be justified in a sexual relationship before they were married.

So far as I know, God has always restricted the sexual relationship to marriage. Marriage always requires a ceremony in which the couple openly acknowledges to other people (witnesses) that they intend, beginning with that event, to be man and wife. It never is simply a private sexual act between just the two of them – that is fornication.

Note that, later in chapter 4, Boaz declared before the elders and the whole city his intent to marry Ruth, and the elders declared themselves to be witnesses. Then she became his wife and he went in to her so she conceived (4:9,10,13). To go in to her before marriage would be fornication – Hebrews 13:4; 1 Corinthians 7:2-5. (And remember that, before Boaz met with the other near kinsman, he and Ruth did not know if they ever would marry.)

It is clear from the story as it proceeds that there was no sexual relationship in this event. Instead, Ruth lay at Boaz' feet until morning. If a woman was seeking to seduce a man, why would she lie down his feet? That would hardly be a chosen position from which to seduce a man.

Furthermore, the entire context of the story emphasizes that all the people involved were godly, upright people. Naomi suggested the act. And Boaz and Ruth were both known for their moral uprightness. Note verse 11 where, in this very context, Boaz

Study Notes on Joshua and Ruth

acknowledges Ruth to be a virtuous woman. In verse 10 he immediately brings God into the very situation, pronouncing a blessing on her for her uprightness. So they both believed they were doing right before God.

On the other hand, why did Naomi even suggest such an approach? Why did Naomi and Ruth not simply openly – perhaps even publicly – approach Boaz and ask him to do the role of a near kinsman? The passage does not explain, so I can only offer my suggestions.

The situation involves customs we don't understand because we do not have the same practice today (compare to the taking off the sandal in 4:8). Naomi said Boaz would understand why Ruth did as she did, and he did understand and immediately responded accordingly. We don't understand, so apparently customs were involved that were known then but not now. (Could lying at his feet symbolize being subject to him and under his protection?)

It may be that Naomi did not want to openly approach Boaz in case Boaz was not willing to perform the duty of a near kinsman. It was possible for the near kinsman to refuse at the cost of personal embarrassment. If this happened, it would not solve Ruth's problem, and it would subject both Boaz and Ruth to public embarrassment. Though Naomi knew Boaz to be a good man, that did not necessarily mean he would want to marry Ruth.

And there was the especially complicating factor that Ruth was a Moabite woman. This could be a great hindrance to any man, especially in light of the prohibition against marrying outside the nation of Israel. We have discussed the fact that marriage to Ruth would be legitimate, since she had converted to the true God (see notes on chapter 1). Nevertheless, there might have been social stigma or other hindrance to such a union in Boaz' mind.

Of course, it is possible that Naomi had some other idea in mind that I have not thought of. In any case, I believe that these possible explanations show that the matter may be properly explained without any suggestion of sexual immorality.

3:10,11 – Boaz pronounced a blessing on Ruth as a virtuous woman and gave a favorable response to her request.

Boaz responded to the request of Ruth by pronouncing a blessing upon her and telling her that he was aware that she was a virtuous woman. In fact, he states that all the people in the town were aware of her virtue. This would explain, not only his desire to marry her as a godly wife, but also his knowledge that it would be proper for him to do so.

He states one specific evidence of her uprightness in that she had not followed after young men, poor or rich. The meaning of this is not specifically explained, but perhaps it relates to the role of the near kinsman. Rather than caring kindly for Naomi, and rather than following the rule of marrying a near kinsman to raise up seed to her dead husband, Ruth might have pursued finding some other young man according to her own pleasure. Instead, she remained true to her responsibility to Naomi and to her deceased husband.

Based on his awareness of Ruth's virtue, Boaz assured her that he would comply with her request. He was willing to seek to marry her and fulfill the role of the near kinsman.

3:12,13 – Boaz informed Ruth that there was an even closer relative than he was. He promised to see if that man would marry Ruth, and if not then Boaz would.

Boaz assured Ruth that he was willing to perform the duty of a near kinsman. However, there was someone else who was even more closely related to her than he was, and according to the law that man had to be given the first opportunity to redeem the property and marry her.

So, Boaz called upon Ruth to lie down and remain at his feet until morning (probably because it would not be wise or safe for her to go home by herself in the dark). Then he would check with this other relative to see if he was willing to perform the duty of a close relative. If so, the matter would be resolved in that way. But if the other man was not willing to perform the duty of a near relative, Boaz gave her his word before the Lord that he would be willing to do so.

3:14,15 – In the morning Boaz sent Ruth home with a generous gift of barley.

Ruth remained at Boaz' feet until morning, as he had instructed. Note that this position assures us that nothing immoral occurred. But they arose early in the morning before it was light enough outside for other people to recognize one another.

Boaz made sure that no one would know that a woman had come to the threshing floor that night. The reason is not explained, but presumably it was to protect Ruth. Nothing immoral had happened, as they both knew, but he wanted to make sure that her reputation was protected. If other people observed, they probably would not understand the reasons for what happened. And Boaz probably would not make the circumstances known until after he had talked to the other near kinsman.

Study Notes on Joshua and Ruth

Before she left, he gave her a gift. He told her to hold out the shawl that she had been wearing, and he filled it with six measures of barley. She then took this with her to the city. The word "ephah" was added by the translators. The Waldrons suggest that would be too great an amount for Ruth to have carried in her shawl. Apparently, we do not know exactly what size the measure was, however it was a generous gift.

3:16-18 – When Ruth returned home, Naomi assured her that Boaz would seek to resolve the matter that day.

Ruth then returned to Naomi and told her all that happened. She showed Naomi the gift of barley, explaining that Boaz had told her not to go home empty-handed to Naomi. All this reassured Naomi that Boaz was serious and would pursue the matter diligently. She urged Ruth to wait patiently till they learned the outcome (no doubt patience would be required for someone waiting to hear the outcome of whom she would marry). She was confident that Boaz would not rest until the matter had been resolved even that very day.

Ruth Chapter 4

Chapter 4 - Ruth and Boaz Marry.

4:1,2 – Boaz met with the other close relative and with the elders of the city.

As Naomi had predicted, Boaz wasted no time meeting with the other near kinsman to make the necessary arrangements. Important matters of business were generally in those days conducted at the gate of the city. People had to come in or go out through the gate, so Boaz would be likely to meet the near kinsman there.

So Boaz went to the gate of the city to wait, and eventually the near kinsman came as Boaz had hoped that he would. Boaz asked him to come aside and sit down. Then he arranged for ten of the elders of the city to come to serve as witnesses to the agreement. The elders were the city leaders. If the arrangement was made in their presence, then there would be qualified witnesses whom no one could dispute.

4:3,4 – Boaz began by discussing the redemption of the property that had belonged to Naomi's husband. The near kinsman said he would redeem it.

Boaz informed the other near kinsman that Naomi had returned from Moab and had sold a piece of property that had belonged to her husband Elimelech. As discussed earlier, the close relatives would have the right to redeem the property. So, Boaz informed the relative of his right to buy back the property that had belonged to Naomi's husband.

He asked the kinsman if he wanted to redeem it, which would be his right to do if he so chose. But if he was not willing to redeem it, then Boaz was next in line. The relative said that he was willing to redeem the property.

Study Notes on Joshua and Ruth

4:5,6 – Boaz then informed the relative that he would also be required to perform the role of the near kinsman to Ruth, but the man then refused.

Again, as we have discussed in chapter 3, the near kinsman would also have the responsibility to marry Ruth to raise up an heir to her dead husband. So Boaz informed the relative that, if he chose to buy the field from Naomi, he would also be responsible to perform the role of the near kinsman so that Ruth's dead husband would have an heir to continue his inheritance.

Having heard that, the close relative declined to redeem the inheritance, because he said he would ruin his own inheritance. So he called upon Boaz to redeem it for himself. (I am not clear why the same man must both redeem the property and marry Ruth. Why could not one man do one and another man do the other? Perhaps it was required by the law. Henry suggests that perhaps Naomi tied the two together to be sure Ruth was provided for.)

It is not completely clear to me how it would ruin the man's inheritance to marry Ruth. The Waldron's explain that, if he redeemed the field and married Ruth, Ruth's child would inherit the redeemed property. In that case, the money he spent to redeem the field would actually reduce the inheritance that he would have for his own children. Of course, that would simply be the consequence of fulfilling the responsibility of the near kinsman. But apparently, he was not willing to do so.

In any case, the result was that the opportunity came to Boaz who was next in line. Boaz was not only willing to redeem the property, but he had already agreed that he was willing to marry Ruth if he had the opportunity. It is obvious that he had come to highly respect her. Being an honorable man, he was willing to do what the law expected of him and what, by this time, he apparently desired to do.

4:7,8 – Boaz and the near kinsman then confirmed the arrangement.

The custom in those days was to confirm an agreement of redeeming or exchanging by one man giving his sandal to the other. So the relative took off his sandal and gave it to Boaz. He affirmed that Boaz then had the right to redeem the property and, by implication, to marry Ruth.

Deuteronomy 25:5-9 said, if the near relative would not marry his brother's widow to raise up an heir to the dead brother, the woman should remove his sandal and spit in his face as a sign of humiliation. But here it appears that the exchanging of the sandal was a way of confirming any act of redemption or exchange.

Perhaps the removal of the sandal in Deuteronomy 25 was a sign that formalized his refusal to marry the woman, as in other agreements, but the spitting in his face was what humiliated him.

In this case there was no need to humiliate the man, since he and Boaz had both agreed on an alternative arrangement to provide for the redemption and the inheritance.

4:9,10 – Boaz called upon the elders and the people to witness his purchase of Naomi's property and his agreement to marry Ruth.

These verses explain why Boaz called the elders to be present when he met with the near relative. He called upon the elders and the people to witness the transaction that had been completed. He said they were witnesses that he had purchased all that had belonged to Naomi's husband Elimelech and to Naomi's dead sons Chilion and Mahlon. He had redeemed their property.

In addition he had acquired Ruth, who was the widow of Mahlon, to be his wife. He reminded them all that this was according to the law, so he could perpetuate the inheritance of those who had died, that their inheritance would not be cut off among the people. This explains again the purpose of the law of the near relative marrying the widow of one who died without descendant.

Note that the people were witnesses, not just to the land transfer, but also to the intent to marry. A couple is not married just because they have a sexual union. This example shows that first there is an open declaration before witnesses that they intend to be man and wife. Then they become man and wife and they have the marriage relationship – verse 13. To have the sexual union before marriage is fornication – Hebrews 13:4.

4:11,12 – The people not only witnessed the transaction, they also pronounced a blessing upon Boaz and Ruth.

The people and the elders at the gate agreed that they were witnesses to the transaction. But their response also shows that they knew there was more to this than simply a legal transaction. They pronounced a blessing upon Boaz and Ruth in their marriage. They expressed the hope that Ruth would be like Rachel and Leah, the wives of Jacob through whom the nation of Israel had begun.

They called upon him to prosper and become famous in the city of Bethlehem. Then they expressed the desire that his offspring through Ruth would cause his house to become like that of Perez, the son that Tamar bore to Judah.

Judah, of course, was the head of their own tribe, since they were of the tribe of Judah. And Tamar had born Perez to Judah in fulfillment of the law that the widow should raise up seed to her dead husband (albeit carried out in an immoral manner in that case). Boaz was in turn a descendant of Perez (verses 18ff), so it was appropriate to name Perez as an example of what they wished for Boaz.

This response shows that they had great respect for Boaz and had developed a great respect for Ruth. They saw in this marriage what we also ought to see in it as an expression of the beauty of the bond of matrimony between two godly people. And they saw it as a blessing, not just to the men who had died, but also to Ruth and Boaz.

4:13,14 – Ruth then gave birth to a son, and the women of the city pronounced a blessing on Naomi.

So Boaz and Ruth became man and wife, and in this marriage relationship they gave birth to a son. Any child would have been a great blessing, but in this case it was a special blessing to have a son to carry on the family name and inheritance. (Note that they became man and wife first, then he went in to her, not the other way around – see notes on verse 10.)

Notice how God had blessed Ruth for her virtues. She had been a poor, childless widow from a foreign country. She had endured the lowly task of gleaning behind the servants in the fields of the rich man Boaz. Now she was Boaz' wife and mistress of his fields and servants. Further, she had a son who would eventually give them descendants of the greatest importance in the nation and the history of the world.

Then the women pronounced a blessing upon Naomi, that the Lord had not left her without a close relative. They called upon his name to be famous in Israel. Verse 15 shows that this refers primarily to the child that was born.

4:15,16 – Ruth and her son were a great blessing to Naomi in her old age, and Naomi became a nurse to the child.

This child who had been born would be a restorer of life and a nourisher of Naomi's old age. Notice the people recognized this was a blessing, not just to Ruth and Boaz, but also to Naomi. Without Ruth and Boaz, Naomi would have been left, not only without descendant, but also without a family of any kind. She would have no one to take care of her in her old age. But now her future care seemed to be assured. It was as though she had been restored to life that she had lost.

They specifically praised Ruth as the one who brought this about. Having obtained a godly husband who would provide for Ruth and Naomi, and having brought a child to be a descendant, Ruth had shown faithfulness to Naomi better than many sons would have done. So the women said that Ruth had been better to Naomi than seven sons.

Then we are told that Naomi took the child and held him to her bosom and became a nurse to him. I assume this means that she helped bring him up and care for him.

Notice how God had blessed Naomi for her virtues. She had been a childless widow living in abject poverty. Because of God's blessings to her through Ruth, she now had a family to care for her, a secure future, and a grandson to love and care for. She had a descendant to secure her husband's inheritance and to in turn give other descendants who would be among the greatest men of history.

4:17-22 – The child who was born to Ruth and Boaz was named Obed, the grandfather of king David.

Apparently the custom in those days was for neighbors to suggest a name for a child who was born. So in saying that a son – that is an offspring – had been born to Naomi, they gave him the name of Obed. The name means one who serves; and as we have seen, Obed would become important as a blessing to Naomi and the family.

The story then closes by telling us that Obed was the father of Jesse, who was in turn the father of David, one of the greatest kings that Israel ever had. We are then given a genealogy from Perez, the son of Judah, all the way down through David. Note that the genealogy lists Boaz as the father of Obed. So that even though Obed was the legal heir of Naomi's son, he was also the legal heir of Boaz.

This shows that the story was not just an account of a lovely romance, though it certainly was that. It was not just an account of God's blessings upon a needy and godly family, though it certainly was that. Nor is it even just a story showing the importance of the family bond, though it is certainly that. More important, it is a record of how God brought into the world the line of David, which became the line of the kings that ruled over Israel.

No doubt this was the important point to those who would have read the book in the Old Testament. But for those of us who know the rest of the story, there is an even greater significance, because David was the ancestor of Jesus Christ. So this story, like so many others in the Old Testament, becomes especially important to us because of its relationship to our salvation through Jesus. This story

Study Notes on Joshua and Ruth

shows the plan of God in bringing into the world the one who would be the great ancestor of our Lord and Master. As such, it serves a major role in the Bible story.

Ruth had made great sacrifices to serve God. She had left her family, her homeland, and her culture, including her gods. She had lived in poverty and hardship. She could never have known at that time the great blessings God had in store for her. Yet through her, God gave mankind a great dynasty of kings and ultimately the Savior of the world. But she first had to be willing to make great sacrifice for Him.

We too may never know what good God has in store for us. We will not be ancestors of Christ, but we may be the means to bring great blessings – including the blessing of salvation – to our children and many others. And ultimately He has promised us eternal life. But we must first be willing to pay whatever price is necessary to serve Him faithfully.

Sources Frequently Cited in These Notes

Free, Joseph P., *Archaeology and Bible History*, (11th edition); Scripture Press Publications, Wheaton, IL, 1972

Henry, Matthew, *Matthew Henry's Commentary on the Whole Bible*; reprinted by Sovereign Grace Publishers, Wilmington, DE, 1972 (original is public domain)

Horne, Thomas, *Introduction to the Critical Study and Knowledge of the Holy Scriptures*, 4 volumes; T. Cadwell, Strand, London, 1828 (public domain)

Keil, C. F. and Franz Delitzsch, *Commentary on the Old Testament;* originally published by T. and T. Clark, Edinburgh, 1866-1891 (public domain)

Millard, Alan, *Nelson's Illustrated Wonders and Discoveries of the Bible;* Thomas Nelson Pub., Nashville, TN, 1997

Pfeiffer, Charles F., *Baker's Bible Atlas*, Baker Book House, Grand Rapids, MI, 1961

Waldron, Bob and Sandra; *In the Days of the Judges: Conquest of the Land and the Period of the Judges*, Bob Waldron, Athens, Alabama, 1996

Printed books, booklets, and tracts available at
www.gospelway.com/sales
Free Bible study articles online at
www.gospelway.com
Free Bible courses online at
www.biblestudylessons.com
Free class books at
www.biblestudylessons.com/classbooks
Free commentaries on Bible books at
www.biblestudylessons.com/commentary
Contact the author at
www.gospelway.com/comments
Free e-mail Bible study newsletter –
www.gospelway.com/update_subscribe.htm

Study Notes on Joshua and Ruth

Made in the USA
Coppell, TX
03 February 2020